Volume, aerial biomass, and carbon content for *Pinus occidentalis*, *Pinus caribaea* var. Caribaea, *Swietenia mahagoni* and *Swietenia macrophylla*

Santiago Wigberto Bueno López

Pontificia Universidad Catolica Madre y Maestra
Santiago de los Caballeros
Dominican Republic

July 28th, 2019

DEDICATION

To Leia, Luis and Braude

CONTENTS

ACKNOWLEDGMENTS

We are thankful to all technical personnel from Plan Sierra and PISACC, for their selfless support. We are also grateful to the administrative staff of the Pontificia Universidad Catolica Madre y Maestra, specially Niulka Martinez and Carla Urbaéz. The Applied Research Program on Silviculture, Environment and Climate Change (PISACC) from the Pontificia Universidad Católica Madre and Maestra (PUCMM) conducted the overall coordination of this study under the coordination of Santiago W. Bueno-Lopez, Ph.D. with the assistance of the Luis Rene Caraballo and Miriam Dominguez. The Research Unit of Plan Sierra, coordinated by Alfredo Jiménez, M.Sc., carried out fieldwork. In the task force in charge of fieldwork were, Juan Gilberto Torres Herrera, Eugenio Agramonte, Nelson Santelises, Ramón Serrata, Jesus Rodriguez and José Reyes.

Summary

To assess biomass and carbon stored and at the same time, and to develop allometric models of main species used by Plan Sierra as pillars of their reforestation programs, 52 forest stands were inventoried: 15 of *Pinus caribaea* var. Caribaea; 15 of *Pinus occidentalis*; 13 of *Swietenia mahagoni* (Small leave mahagoni); and 9 of *Swetenia macrophylla* (Honduran mahogany). A study protocol was developed to include a specific number of trees in each of six age classes. There were difficulties in locating representative trees for each class and the destructive sampling was not executed according to the established plan.

Fifty-two forest stands were characterized in terms of silvicultural and allometric attributes. Assessed forest stands have on average, 19, 19, 23 and 16 years for *P. occidentalis, P. caribaea var.* Caribaea*; S. mahagoni* and S. macrophylla, respectively. In terms of area, they were established on 1.64, 2.47, 1.52 and 1.55 hectares, following the same species order. The number of trees per hectare was 273, 586, 543 and 436. Tree volume including bark was in the order of 37.72, 130.00, 36.6 and 45.16 cubic meters. Discriminating by age, average dbh (cm) was 18.52, 20.05, 16.68 and 14.13. Average total height in meters (m) was 15.91, 14.80, 9.94, 7.72.

Regarding the individually sampled trees, average aerial total carbon (Kg) per tree was 86.99, 53.26, 37.74, and 35.05. Within forest stands, aerial total carbon in Kg per hectare was 44,064.41; 78,071.72; 23,949.15 and 45,188.64. Average CO_2_equivalente (Kg/ha) was 161,727.40; 286,523.21; 87,893.40 and 165,842.29. The species with the greatest amount of carbon captured at the stand level is *P. caribaea*, with 86.99 Kg per tree. Individually, the content of carbon, derived by multiplying dry biomass by carbon concentration, is greater in *P. caribaea*, and therefore the amount of CO_2 equivalent captured by this species is higher on average (365.81 kg).

Analysis of variance (Table 24) shows that carbon content in branches is statistically significant and greater in *P. occidentalis* than the carbon content in the same tissue of both mahogany species, although its biomass is lower than in *P. caribaea*. Carbon content in *P. caribaea* branches is statistically significant and larger than in S. macrophylla. Foliage of *P. occidentalis* has higher carbon content than the equivalent tissue in S. macrophylla. A plausible reason is that, for the same age class, trees in stands evaluated for *P. caribaea* are on average larger than the other species, with dbh and total H averaging 20.05 cm and 15.91 m, respectively.

Individually consideration of the 52 sampled trees shows that, stem density averaged at three relative heights (0.1, 0.5 and 0.8) was respectively 0.48, 0.44, 0.58, and 0.52 for *P. occidentalis*, *P. caribaea*, *S. mahagoni* and *S. macrophylla*, respectively. For the same species order, dry-weight / fresh-weight relationship in the stem was 0.52, 0.46, 0.64 and 0.59. In branches, samples taken at three positions within the crown had a dry-weight / fresh-weight ratio of 0.48, 0.49, 0.53 and 0.53, respectively. Within the foliage, this ratio was 0.47, 0.49, 0.46 and 0.46.

For *P. occidentalis* sampled trees, the average global amounts for all variables including DAP, aerial total dry biomass (Kg), total carbon (Kg) and CO_2_equivalente (Kg) were, respectively: 19.82, 15.13, 152.96, 59.67 and 218.99. In *P. caribaea* the corresponding quantities were: 23.76, 18.51, 287.71, 149.39 and 548.28. In *S. mahagoni*, 15.51, 8.54, 122.91, 48.63 and 189.28. In *S. macrophylla*: 16.37, 10.97, 132.05, 51.57 and 189.28.

It was expected to find a positive increase in biomass with respect to age, however, the "sample" located trees are not representative of all the variability in terms of dimensionality for different age classes. The amount of biomass accumulated and therefore carbon captured is directly proportional to the size of the tree.

In case of *P. occidentalis* a single tree represented age class 7. This tree is smaller in terms of dimensions to the average number of trees in the age class 6, with a dbh of 21 cm and a total height of 14,65 m, while the average of these variables for age class 6 is of 24.5 cm and 18.17 m respectively. In addition, the dimensions in age class 5 were higher than age class 6.

Individual consideration of the 52 trees shows that, stem density averaged at three relative heights (0.1, 0.5 and 0.8) was respectively 0.48, 0.44, 0.58, and 0.52. The relationship dry-weight / fresh-weight in the stem was 0.52, 0.46, 0.64, and 0.59, respectively. In branches, samples taken at three positions within the canopy had a dry-weight / fresh-weight relationship of 0.48 0.49 0.53 and 0.53 respectively. In the foliage this ratio was 0.49, 0.46, 0.46, and 0.47.

For *P. occidentalis* sample trees of, the average global amounts by age class of dbh (cm), H (m), aerial dry biomass (kg), aerial total C content, (kg) and the CO_2_equivalente (kg) were, respectively: 19.82, 15.13, 152.96, 59.67 and 218.99. For *P. caribaea* these quantities were: 23.76, 18.51, 287.71, 149.39 and 548.28. In *S. mahagoni* 15.51, 8.54, 122.91, 48.63 and 189.28. For *S. mahagoni* 16.37, 10.97, 132.05, 51.57 and 189.28.

We anticipated finding an increase in biomass positively correlated with age; however, the "sample" trees assessed are not representative of all the variability in terms of age class. The amount of biomass accumulated and therefore carbon captured is directly proportional to the size of the tree.

In addition to evaluating biomass and carbon in the species, different relationships including, those between dbh, total tree height and volume including bark of trees sampled in temporary plots were considered. The relationship between dbh and H is better described by a logarithmic relationship. The best fit for dbh vs H is found *for P. caribaea*, followed by *S. macrophylla*, *P. occidentalis*, and lastly for *S. mahagoni*.

To develop the allometric models, four models were fitted in order to establish the relationship between the dependent variable 'aerial total carbon' and the predicting variables, dbh, H and dbh2H. For each type of model the method of least squares was employed, by applying logarithmic transformations, which allows to correct the problem of linearity and heteroscedasticity inherent to this type of biological variables. The inverse exponential function was used to express models developed in original scale units of the data.

Recommended models to estimate aerial total carbon in the species evaluated, based on the fitting and age classes studied are as follows: For *P. occidentalis*, model [1.1]; For *P. caribaea*, model [4.1]; For *S. mahagoni*, model [6.1]; For S. macrophylla, models [8.1] and [10.1]. Models containing a single independent variable are [1.1], [4.1], [6.1] and [8.1]. They are simpler and easily applied.

The results of Goodness-of-Fit statistical tests (Table 33) show that the allometric equations developed allow adequate predictions, and that the best predictor of the dependent variable, carbon content, is diameter at breast height (dbh) of the tree at 1.30 meters above ground.

1 Introduction

To understand the carbon cycle, particularly the impacts of human activities on the accumulation and flow of carbon dioxide (CO_2) from and towards natural deposits, is critical for tackling climate change. Main challenge to overcome in the first instance, it is the development of the necessary tools for a correct quantification and monitoring of CO_2, considered to be the main greenhouse gas from anthropogenic origins.

To quantify carbon storage in forest biomass within the area of influence of Plan Sierra, an NGO that has been working continuously since 1980 in the restoration of forest ecosystems in La Sierra, Dominican Republic, we selected the main four timber species used by this organization in its reforestation efforts. Volume, aerial biomass, and carbon for each of them, discriminating by age class were assessed to develop allometric equations throughout the age range. The species selected by technical staff of Plan Sierra were, *Pinus occidentalis*, *Pinus caribaea* var. Caribaea, *Swietenia mahagoni* and *Swietenia macrophylla*.

Biomass and carbon are key factors in the estimation of the contribution of forest ecosystems in the carbon cycle (Picard et al., 2012). Allometric equations to predict the biomass and carbon in a tree, starting from easily measurable dendrometric characteristics, such as height or diameter, are very common (Dickinson and Zenner, 2010). Once developed, they have the advantage of providing a rapid method for estimating biomass carbon content, avoiding the need for costly destructive sampling.

Canga et al. (2013) report that the first studies to estimate biomass productivity of certain species were those carried out by Burger (1945, 1953) in *Larix decidua* and *Picea abies*. These authors point out further investigations focused on the allocation of dry weight in tree components.

Navar (2014) classifies allometric equations of aboveground biomass, depending on the spatial scale at which trees are harvested: (1) local equations specific to a site, focused on a single species in a small area; (2) general equations specific to a site developed for individual species, not limited by geographical boundaries; and (3) regional equations covering all species of trees within an ecosystem.

However, Fonseca et al. (2012) and Chaturvedi and Raghubanshi (2015), point out that errors occur when researchers applied the allometric equations outside areas where they were developed, considering that different soil and environmental conditions, stand structure, species composition, and other key factors may prevail. In addition, different species have different architecture and average density of wood; therefore, it would be desirable to develop species-specific allometric equations, reducing the uncertainty due to the variation among species.

In terms of the carbon content, the importance of forests as carbon sinks (C) is directly related to the content of biomass (IPCC, 2003). As in the case of biomass, research studies on the contents of C in trees, have been fully made. Thomas and Martin (2011, 2012) assessed and summarized the efforts of research on carbon contained in tropical trees and found only a small number of studies where specific carbon fraction has been incorporated. These authors also emphasize another concern, and that is the assumption that the biomass consists of 50% of carbon on a mass-mass basis, which is not real. Recent studies indicate that the assumption of 50% has about 5% errors in estimates of forest carbon stocks and that conifers tend to have significantly higher C content than angiosperms.

Gifford (2000) estimated a C concentration figure of 50.5% of biomass in species of eucalyptus and 54.1% for *Pinus Radiata*. Lamlom and Savidge (2003) reported a 51.5 C content % in conifers against a 48.4% in angiosperms, while Thomas and Malczewski (2007) published 50.9% vs 49.6% in conifers and angiosperms, respectively. Lamlom and Savidge (2003) assert the highest content of C for conifers may be due to the higher content of lignin, with approximate values around 30% compared with 20% of angiosperms vs conifers, respectively.

In a study conducted by Bueno-López et al. (in print, 2013) it was found that *P. occidentalis* C concentration (%) on average (48 trees), within present study area, was higher in the foliage (49.8%), followed by the branches (46.37%) and, finally, the stem (45.95%). On average, each individual tree stored 0.175 tons of aerial total C.

The absence of reliable data as to C concentration of species in tropical forests based on chemical analysis has been considered as a breach in terms of relevant information necessary to resolve (Elias and Potvin 2003; IPCC, 2006), to reduce the error associated with the estimated carbon sequestration of forest species (Fu et al., 2013).

1.1 Objectives

- Silvicultural and biometrical characterization of forest at 52 sampling points allocated for the development of the study.

- Application of a destructive sampling method to evaluate volume of individual trees selected at each point of sampling according to methodology proposed.

- Obtain and analyze sub-samples to quantify wood basic density and C fraction of trees selected.

- Fit regression models and select the best equation for predicting volume, estimate biomass and C stock at individual trees level.

2 Materials an Methods
2.1 Study area

The study area is the zone of influence of the NGO Plan Sierra. It has an extension of 177, 898 hectares. It is enclosed within the following geographic coordinates: 19 ° 39' 36" - 18 ° 57' 36" north latitude and 70 ° 39' 00" - 71 ° 21' 36" West longitude. This region includes the municipalities of San Ignacio de Sabaneta, Santiago, San José de Las Matas, Moncion and Janico. There are seven (7) watersheds, thirty-seven (37) micro basins and six (6) protected areas.

Since the 1980, many families from the villages of Jánico, San José de Las Matas, El Rubio and other communities dedicated this piece of land to livestock production. Many emigrated to the United States. This, in addition to the ecosystem restoration activities of Plan Sierra, is the main reason behind the significant changes experienced in the changed observed of increased forest cover and better use of soil resources.

The study area presents various types of lives zones, according to Holdrige (1987) denomination. They range from dry forest to very humid forest, with precipitation oscillating from 545 mm to more than 2,000 mm per year and a temperature average of 26 °C. Topography is mostly stepped with slopes ranging from 0% to 64% and greater. According to a study of productive capacity of soils (OAS, 1965), soils are found from class IV to VII, whose proper uses should be forestry.

For the most part of the last century, this area was under an intense activity linked mostly to growing cattle, penetrating even within the Armando Bermudez National Park. Another traditional activity is the production of coffee, distributed in most of the northern slopes between Cerro Prieto, Las Lagunas, Juncalito, Diferencia and Manaclas; Coffee plantations are also present in Los Ramones, Jicomé, El Aguacate, El Gallo and La Leonor.

Areas planted with the species studied here (Figure 1) include: fifteen stands of *P. occidentalis*; fifteen stands for *P. caribaea*; thirteen stands for *S. mahagoni*; and nine stands for *S. macrophylla*.

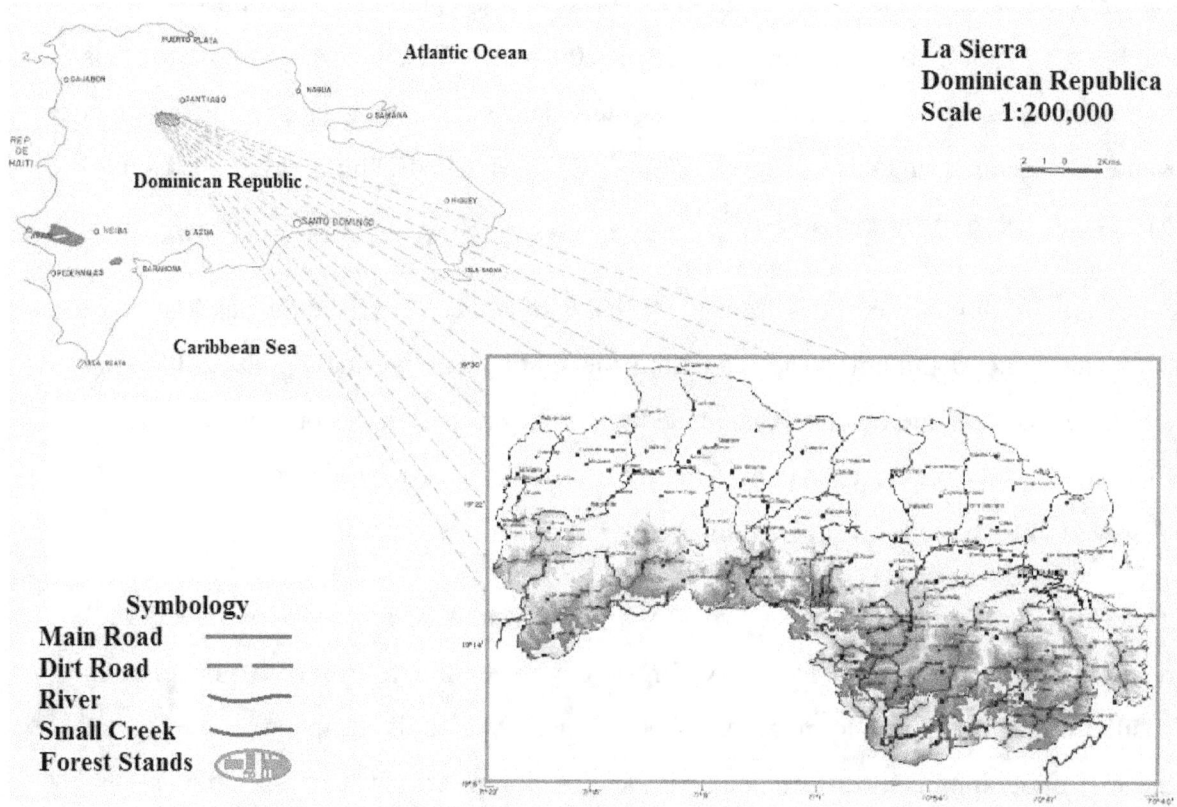

Figure 1. Localization of forest stands evaluated for *P. occidentalis*, *P. caribaea*, *S. mahagoni* and *S. macrophylla*, within Plan Sierra area.

2.2 Characterization of the collected sample basis: forest inventory

Firstly, we proceeded to find in the field stands with appropriate age as required for the study. The interest was to find a representative tree to be evaluated for biomass and carbon content in each stand. The stands should be located in a wide spectrum of geographic variation, trying different life zone areas. Age classes of interest for the four species were as follows: Age Class 1: 0 - 5 years; age class 2: 6 - 10 years; age class 3: 11 - 15 years; age class 4: 16 - 20 years; age class 5: 21 - 25 years; age class 6: 26 - 30 years; age class 7: 31 - 35 years. It was assumed that not all age classes would be present for some of the species. Once the stands were located, a forest inventory was conducted for characterization. Table 1 shows the planned distribution of trees by each class for the destructive phase of the study. Pertinent summary information of the inventory process will be presented ahead.

Table 1. Destructive sampling for biomass and carbon content assessment within planted areas of the Plan Sierra.

Species		AGE CLASS (YEARS)						
		0 - 5	6 - 10	11 - 15	16 - 20	21 - 25	26 - 30	Total
		No. Trees						
P. occidentalis	Sampled Trees	2	2	2	3	3	3	15
P. caribaea		2	2	2	3	3	3	15
S. macrophylla		2	2	2	2	2	0	10
S. mahagoni		2	2	2	3	3	3	15

2.3 Sampling and analytical process

In each forest stand circular plots of 350 m2 were established in each center of the selected stand. In each plot, all trees were identified and measurements of diameter at the height (dbh at 1.30 m above ground) and total height (H in m) of representative trees was recorded. We computed stand density (trees / has) and basal area per hectare (BA, m2 / has). A single tree was selected per plot and 52 representative trees were destructively sampled.

Trees were felled as closely as possible to the ground (~ 10 cm). After felling, we measured tree total height (H) to the nearest centimeter, the diameter and bark thickness were measured to the nearest cm in the stump and every two meters to a minimum top diameter of 4 cm, for pine species. In case of the mahoganies, measurements were made at one and two meters, depending on the total height of the tree. To section each tree in the different components, the branches were cut at its intersection with the main stem and foliage with twigs with a maximum thickness of 1 cm in diameter.

Main stem of large trees was cut into logs of varied length, to a minimum top diameter of 4 cm. Green weight of each component in the field, was determined using appropriate heavy duty scales. In selected trees, sawdust from the cuts was weighed, in order to estimate its weight base on diameter and species to addition it to the weight of the stem. To that end we employed simple linear regression equations, verifying the relationship between weight and diameter at each cut.

Subsamples from the main steam including bark were taken in the form of 5 cm thick disks at relative heights of 0.1, 0.5 and 0.8 in relation to total tree height. From branches, three subsamples were taken at the bottom, the middle and upper portions of the canopy. Furthermore, subsamples of foliage from the upper, medium and lower portions of the canopy were also taken. All of the tissues from this stage were weighed for the determination of green weight with high precision scales. For the determination of biomass, all tissues sampled were coded, placed in Ziploc bags and transported to the laboratory for further processing.

In the lab, samples were oven-dried at approximate temperatures of 110 ° C for 24 hours, until constant weight was achieved. After drying, dry weight was measured, prior to the determination of dry-weight / green-weight ratio for each subsample by component. The dry biomass of each component (stem plus bark, branches and foliage) was calculated using the following relationship.

$$B_i = B_{Gi} \cdot \frac{S_i}{S_{Gi}}$$

where Bi = is the total dry biomass for component i; BGi = total green weight of tissue component i; Si = subsample dry weight for component i; and SGi = subsample fresh weight for component i.

2.4 Carbon content

To estimate the carbon content in tissues, subsamples at different relative heights within the stem, and in different positions of the canopy for branches and foliage, were obtained. For each subsample already dried in the oven, the carbon concentration was determined using weights of approximately 50 mg in a Rapid CS cube (manufactured by Elementar Analysensysteme GmbH). This latest generation instrument converts carbon compounds by oxidation at 950 ° C to carbon dioxide (CO_2), which it is measured by infrared detection.

2.5 Allometric Models

2.5.1 Graphic exploration of the data

As a first step in the development of predictive models, we visually assessed the relationships between the dependent variable, aerial total dry biomass (BT); and common predictor variables, dbh, H, and dbh2H, to be able to specify the error form between these variables, the mean and variance relationship. Scatterplot graphs were constructed to determine the nature of these relationships. If the residues were not constants (presence of heteroscedasticity), a power model would be adopted to link the variation of residuals to the effect variable included in the model.

2.5.2 Model fit

Four different types of models were adjusted to establish the relationship between the predictor variables and the dependent variable (Table 2). For each type of model, the method of least squares was used by applying logarithmic transformations, which allows to correct the problem of linearity and heteroscedasticity in case that these problems were present. The inverse exponential function returns the model so that it can be applied to the original data.

Table 2. Model types fitted by logarithmic transformation.

Model	Model Form	Variance Form	Method
[A]	$ln(CT) = \beta_0 + \beta_1\, ln(DAP) + \varepsilon$	$Var(\varepsilon) = \sigma^2$	
[B]	$ln(CT) = \beta_0 + \beta_1\, ln(DAP^2 H) + \varepsilon$	$Var(\varepsilon) = \sigma^2$	**Least**
[C]	$ln(CT) = \beta_0 + \beta_1\, ln(DAP) + ln(DAP)^2 + \varepsilon$	$Var(\varepsilon) = \sigma^2$	**Squares**
[D]	$ln(CT) = \beta_0 + \beta_1\, ln(DAP) + ln(H) + \varepsilon$	$Var(\varepsilon) = \sigma^2$	

Figure 2 shows the process carried out to comply with the objectives of the study of evaluating biomass and carbon sequestration in the four selected species. The descriptive statistics for the sampled tree allometric variables in each species are displayed in Table 3, 4, 5 and 6.

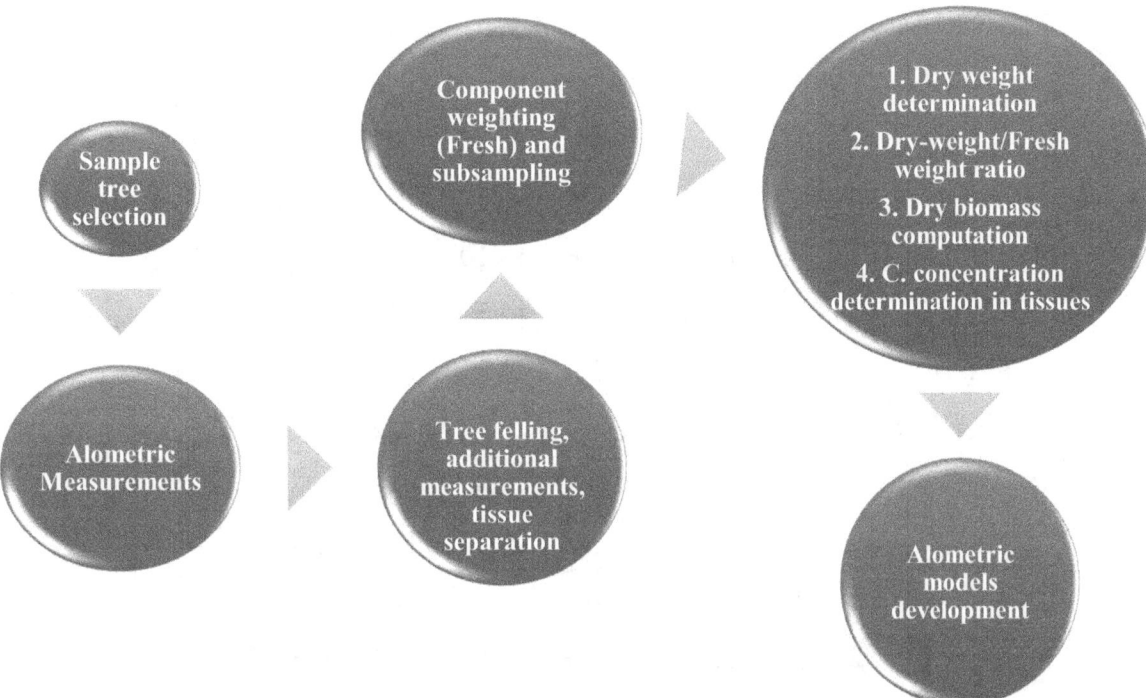

Figure 2. Process for the evaluation of biomass and carbon capture in *P. occidentalis*, *P. caribaea*, *S. mahagoni* and *S. macrophylla*.

Table 3. Descriptive statistics for the allometric variables of sampled trees in each species: *Pinus occidentalis*.

Age	dbh	H	LF	HIC	D-IC	Vcc	Vsc	N Logs
7	10.50	11.50	9.10	3.20	8.80	0.06	0.05	7
7	12.10	10.80	8.53	4.80	9.20	0.06	0.05	7
10	16.50	12.80	10.93	3.30	14.50	0.13	0.11	8
10	10.50	12.25	9.85	4.50	15.20	0.02	0.02	8
12	17.50	8.70	5.72	2.45	8.00	0.14	0.12	7
15	17.00	11.50	8.60	3.35	13.10	0.12	0.11	7
18	15.70	15.60	11.60	3.70	15.50	0.15	0.13	8
20	22.70	15.30	13.15	4.20	20.30	0.32	0.29	9
20	23.50	22.00	20.00	6.60	20.00	0.52	0.46	12
23	19.00	18.17	15.47	9.25	11.50	0.26	0.25	10
25	23.50	21.20	19.24	8.64	18.40	0.45	0.40	10
23	27.00	15.90	14.40	5.10	19.60	0.42	0.40	11
30	27.50	21.80	20.50	14.20	13.80	0.55	0.51	12
30	21.50	14.53	12.20	6.00	15.20	0.22	0.21	8
33	21.00	14.65	12.67	8.13	13.50	0.25	0.24	9

dbh: diameter at breast height in cm (1.3 m above ground); H: Total tree height in m; LF: stem length in m; HIC: Height at crown onset in m; D-IC: diameter at crown onset in cm; Vcc: stem volume including bark in m3; Vsc: stem volume without bark in m3; N Logs: number of logs (2 meters log except the top log).

Table 4. Descriptive statistics for the allometric variables of sampled trees: *Pinus caribaea.*

Age	dbh	H	LF	HIC	D-IC	Vcc	Vsc	N Logs
5	7.40	2.74	2.33	0.40	10.10	0.013	0.010	4
8	13.20	8.75	6.95	3.05	11.50	0.063	0.051	6
9	12.70	11.12	9.05	3.00	11.40	0.080	0.065	7
10	19.40	15.35	13.80	5.00	15.30	0.220	0.192	9
10	17.20	13.90	12.20	6.08	13.20	0.173	0.141	9
15	22.40	13.64	12.32	8.73	14.85	0.249	0.153	9
20	17.50	17.80	15.45	6.60	13.60	0.218	0.184	10
20	21.00	19.45	17.40	8.20	15.10	0.312	0.212	11
22	19.80	19.14	17.20	10.00	10.10	0.293	0.260	11
24	25.50	21.04	19.30	9.32	18.40	0.543	0.397	12
25	30.70	27.30	25.50	18.90	15.50	0.841	0.773	15
23	25.00	18.97	17.40	9.50	17.80	0.490	0.428	11
30	35.00	22.90	22.00	11.40	24.80	1.223	1.123	13
32	23.10	21.10	19.50	11.50	15.80	0.431	0.385	12
32	27.00	22.95	21.40	12.05	18.00	0.635	0.568	13

dbh: diameter at breast height in cm (1.3 m above ground); H: Total tree height in m; LF: stem length in m; HIC: Height at crown onset in m; D-IC: diameter at crown onset in cm; Vcc: stem volume including bark in m3; Vsc: stem volume without bark in m3; N Logs: number of logs (2 meters log except the top log).

Table 5. Descriptive statistics for the allometric variables of sampled trees: *Swietenia mahagoni.*

Age	dbh	H	LF	HIC	DAP-IC	V_CC	V_SC	N Logs
5	5.90	4.52	1.80	1.70	4.70	0.006	0.005	4
7	6.90	6.00	2.90	2.00	6.20	0.011	0.009	6
12	12.50	9.60	6.77	2.15	11.50	0.056	0.048	6
14	14.70	8.07	6.17	1.55	14.20	0.066	0.057	9
17	13.90	10.63	8.72	2.70	14.50	0.083	0.072	7
17	9.50	7.10	4.60	1.80	10.20	0.021	0.017	5
25	14.40	9.60	7.70	2.70	13.20	0.095	0.083	6
31	22.00	10.90	9.13	3.12	19.70	0.200	0.177	7
30	22.50	8.75	6.65	2.75	21.50	0.172	0.152	6
35	24.25	8.00	5.45	1.10	25.00	0.064	0.060	7
35	23.20	10.72	8.45	2.65	22.70	0.175	0.156	7
35	15.80	5.82	4.26	1.15	16.50	0.026	0.298	6
35	34.50	10.55	9.10	2.90	29.00	0.349	0.379	7

dbh: diameter at breast height in cm (1.3 m above ground); H: Total tree height in m; LF: stem length in m; HIC: Height at crown onset in m; D-IC: diameter at crown onset in cm; Vcc: stem volume including bark in m3; Vsc: stem volume without bark in m3; N Logs: number of logs (1 meter log except the top log).

Table 6. Descriptive statistics for the allometric variables of sampled trees: *Swietenia macrophylla.*

Age	dbh	H	LF	HIC	DAP-IC	V_CC	V_SC	N
5	7.6	4.6	3.23	2	6	0.01	0.01	6
5	9.5	8.8	5.2	3.6	7	0.03	0.03	5
12	21.6	11.7	9.8	2.45	21.4	0.18	0.16	7
10	17.3	10.3	8	2.84	17.4	0.1	0.09	6
15	14	13.15	11.3	4.14	13.3	0.12	0.10	8
17	14.7	11.5	9.3	3.25	13.2	0.09	0.08	7
18	16.9	14.2	11.63	6.4	13.1	0.16	0.14	8
20	28.2	18.75	17.45	5.65	24	0.68	0.64	11
20	27.5	13.3	11.3	2.5	24.8	0.32	0.29	8

dbh: diameter at breast height in cm (1.3 m above ground); H: Total tree height in m; LF: stem length in m; HIC: Height at crown onset in m; D-IC: diameter at crown onset in cm; Vcc: stem volume including bark in m3; Vsc: stem volume without bark in m3; N Logs: number of logs (1 meter log except the top log).

3 Results and discussion
3.1 Stand Tables

Below, is a summary of stand tables (Tables 7, 8, 9, and 10) by species in the following order: *P. occidentalis, P. caribaea* var. Caribaea, *S. mahagoni* y *S. macrophylla*. These tables contain information on geographic location, altitude above sea level, stand area, number of trees per hectare, volume per hectare and number of trees within temporary plot.

Statistical summary of critical variables for the forest inventory carried out in each of the temporary plots by species is presented in Table 11. For example, *P. occidentalis* were located at an average altitude above sea level of 602 meters. Average area of the stands for this species was 1.64 hectares; average number of trees in the stand and per hectare was 137 and 273, respectively; and the average volume of the stand and per hectare for this species was 18.86 and 37.72 m3, respectively. In addition to the average, maximum and minimum quantities are presented.

Table 7. Stand table summary for *Pinus occidentalis*.

Stand	Age Years	Latitude	Longitude	Altitude Meters above sea level	Area Ha.	No. Trees Stand	No. Trees Ha.	Stand Volume m3	Volume per Hectare m3	No. of Trees in Plot 350 m
1	7	2133677	294589	511	0.50	243	486	11.66	23.32	17
2	7	2130980	290273	881	0.50	314	629	20.20	40.41	22
3	10	2136530	297082	688	2.00	171	343	16.24	32.48	16
4	10	2149332	267010	356	1.00	57	114	2.36	4.73	13
5	12	2125520	300344	844	2.00	143	286	13.86	27.72	15
6	15	2149359	267057	349	0.50	14	29	2.00	4.00	5
7	18	2148618	267830	382	0.50	200	400	17.79	35.58	16
8	20	2138417	295079	490	1.50	14	29	0.96	1.92	9
9	20	2133425	294842	534	0.40	14	29	2.00	4.00	12
10	23	2131893	295617	608	2.50	29	57	1.92	3.83	18
11	25	274279	2135674	741	3.50	120	240	8.90	17.80	14
12	23	2135371	296111	580	4.50	171	343	56.05	112.11	12
13	30	301387	2125913	833	1.25	143	286	55.30	110.60	10
14	30	2137651	281930	712	1.50	129	257	29.38	58.77	9
15	33	2143627	28697	530	2.50	286	571	44.28	88.56	20

Table 8. Stand table summary for *Pinus caribaea* var Caribaea.

	Age	Latitude	Longitude	Altitude	Area	No. Trees		Stand Volume	Volume per Hectare	No. of Trees in Plot
Stand	Years	UTM Zone: 19-Q		Meters above sea level	Ha.	Stand	Ha.	m3	m3	350 m
1	5	2336940	296879	648	1.50	286	571	2.37	4.73	20
2	8	2136896	292196	695	2.00	357	714	18.35	36.69	25
3	9	2149678	267260	344	8.00	714	1429	42.62	85.25	50
4	10	2136437	297218	603	3.00	214	429	32.19	64.37	15
5	10	2136533	296065	678	3.00	393	786	23.88	47.76	28
6	15	2139629	293895	388	0.52	257	514	71.56	143.13	18
7	20	2143617	286967	568	2.00	329	657	78.92	157.84	23
8	20	2143627	286977	530	2.50	357	714	98.20	196.40	25
9	22	2149675	267128	326	1.50	357	714	74.77	149.54	25
10	24	2149795	267499	363	3.50	214	429	91.93	183.85	15
11	25	2143618	286896	537	1.50	186	371	98.46	196.91	13
12	23	2142078	283958	574	0.50	171	343	71.71	143.41	12
13	30	2137605	294970	584	4.00	57	114	41.61	83.23	4
14	32	2149725	267323	357	1.50	214	429	96.14	192.28	15
15	32	2143628	286906	574	2.00	286	571	129.94	259.88	20

Table 9. Stand table summary for _Swietenia mahagoni_.

	Age	Latitude	Longitude	Altitude	Area	No. Trees		Stand Volume	Volume per Hectare	No. of Trees in Plot
Stand	Years	UTM Zone: 19-Q		Meters above sea level	Ha.	Stand	Ha.	m3	m3	350 m
1	5	2138996	296856	461.00	0.70	257	514	1.16	2.33	18.0
2	7	2139468	296907	606.00	0.10	557	1114	9.06	18.12	39.0
3	12	2146190	308131	333.00	1.50	729	1457	56.35	112.69	51.0
4	14	2143922	287110	555.00	0.75	157	314	2.47	4.95	11.0
5	17	2146158	308200	424.00	0.78	514	1029	27.77	55.53	36.0
6	17	2143635	286134	549.00	0.40	286	571	3.75	7.51	20.0
7	25	2143843	286621	569.00	0.50	300	600	18.56	37.12	21.0
8	31	2128246	297472	881.00	0.97	71	143	16.59	33.19	5.0
9	30	2131458	296609	734.00	1.20	100	200	12.12	24.25	7.0
10	35	2140225	301144	582.00	3.00	143	286	24.06	48.11	10.0
11	35	2140743	310722	398.00	5.00	171	343	31.40	62.79	12.0
12	35	2135212	280582	451.00	2.00	143	286	8.30	16.61	10.0
13	35	2132369	295788	670.00	0.76	100	200	26.57	53.13	7.0

Table 10. Stand table summary for Swetenia macrophylla.

	Age	Latitude	Longitude	Altitude	Area	No. Trees		Stand Volume	Volume per Hectare	No. of Trees in Plot
Stand	Years	UTM Zone: 19-Q		Meters above sea level	has	Stand	Ha.	m3	m3	350 m
1	5	2150599	297732	391	3.50	171	343	1.92	3.84	12
2	5	2126779	300527	789	1.50	214	429	3.61	7.22	15
3	12	2130569	297548	787	0.70	143	286	21.27	42.53	10
4	10	2140981	306076	586	2.00	329	657	39.64	79.27	23
5	15	2146146	308167	383	2.00	471	943	33.15	66.30	33
6	17	2145605	307295	445	2.00	514	1029	40.17	80.33	36
7	18	2149725	2677320	336	1.50	71	143	7.48	14.96	5
8	20	2130197	289830	1017	0.25	100	200	51.95	103.89	7
9	20	2140960	306399	330	0.50	14	29	4.31	8.61	5

Table 11. Summary statistics of critical variables for the forest inventory carried out in each of the temporary plots by species.

| Species | Stats | Altitude | Area | No. Trees | | Stand Volume | Volume per Hectare | No. of Trees in Plot |
		Meters above sea level	Ha.	Stand	Ha.	m3	m3	350 m
	Mean	602	1.64	137	273	18.86	37.72	14
P. occidentalis	Max	881	4.5	314	629	56.05	112.11	22
	Min	349	0.4	14	29	0.96	1.92	5
	Mean	517	2.47	293	586	64.84	129.69	21
P. caribaea	Max	695	8	714	1429	129.94	259.88	50
	Min	326	0.5	57	114	2.37	4.73	4
	Mean	554	1.52	271	543	18.32	36.64	19
S. mahagoni	Max	881	5	729	1457	56.35	112.69	51
	Min	333	0.1	71	143	1.16	2.33	5
	Mean	562	1.55	225	451	22.61	45.22	16
S. macrophylla	Max	1017	3.5	514	1029	51.95	103.89	36
	Min	330	0.25	14	29	1.92	3.84	5

3.2 Box-plots for relevant allometric variables by species

The graphs below (Figures 3) present box-plots corresponding to relevant allometric variables for each species. Box-plots summarize descriptive statistics for each variable, including minimum, maximum, first and third quartile values and the median (second quartile). Panel A corresponds to dbh; panel B is a box-plot for total height (m); panel C corresponds to the length of the stem up to 4 cm upper diameter; and panel D summarizes de diameter (cm) at the unset of the canopy.

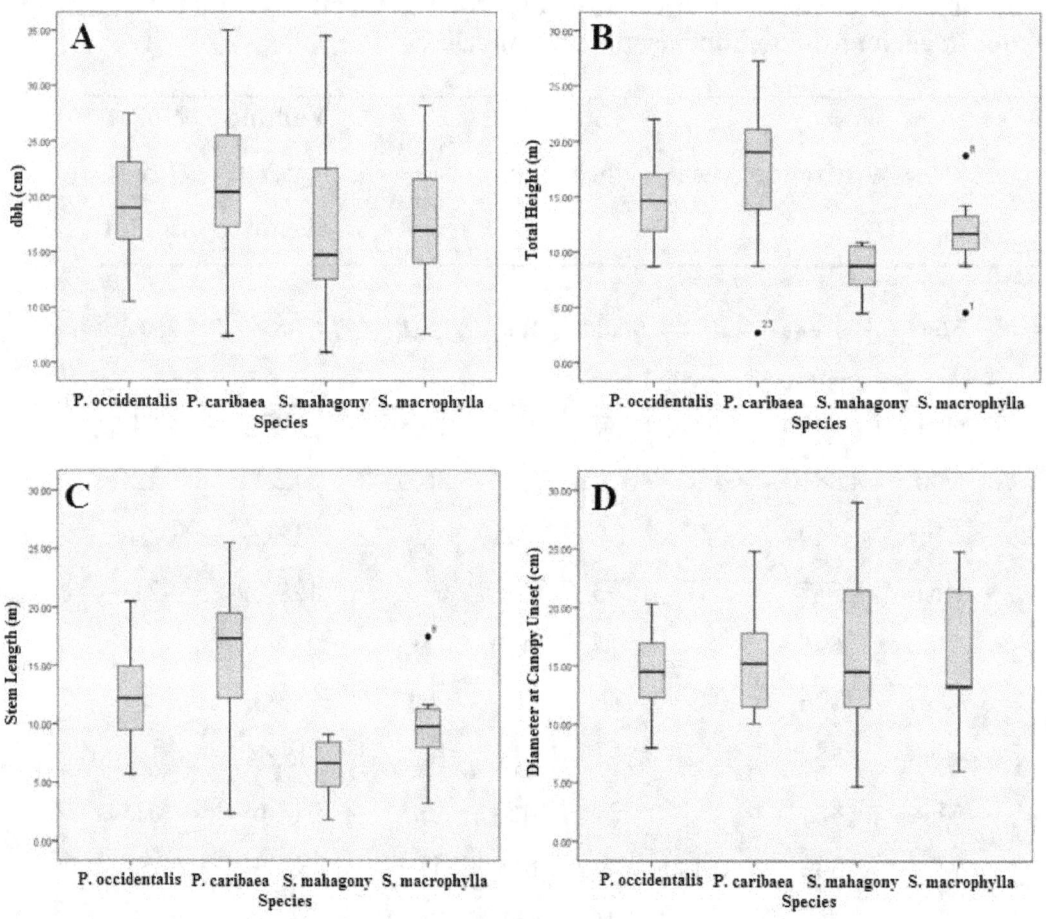

Figure 3. Box-plot graphs for relevant allometric variable by species.

3.3 Relationship between dbh, total height (H) and volume including bark of trees in the temporary plots

The relationship between diameter at breast height (dbh, 1.30 m) and total tree height (H) of signature trees in each of the temporary plots for the four species is shown in Figures 4, 5, 6 and 7 for *P. occidentalis; P. caribaea, S. mahagoni* and *S. macrophylla*, respectively. The relationship between dbh and H are better described by a logarithmic relationship whose equations and coefficients determination are presented in Table 12. Best fit was found for *P. caribaea*, followed by *S. macrophylla*, *P. occidentalis* and finally *S. mahagoni*. The R2 statistic represents the percentage of variation in height, which is explained by the independent variable dbh.

Table 12. Total height equations with their respective coefficient of determination for each species.

Species	Equation	Coefficient of Determination (R2)
P. occidentalis	$H = -9.5048 + 8.3071\ ln(dbh)$	$R^2 = 0.66$
P. caribaea	$H = -18.954 + 12.097\ ln(dbh)$	$R^2 = 0.72$
S. mahagoni	$H = 0.5143 + 2.9579\ ln(dbh)$	$R^2 = 0.54$
S. macrophylla	$H = -6.3209 + 6.3455\ ln(dbh)$	$R^2 = 0.71$

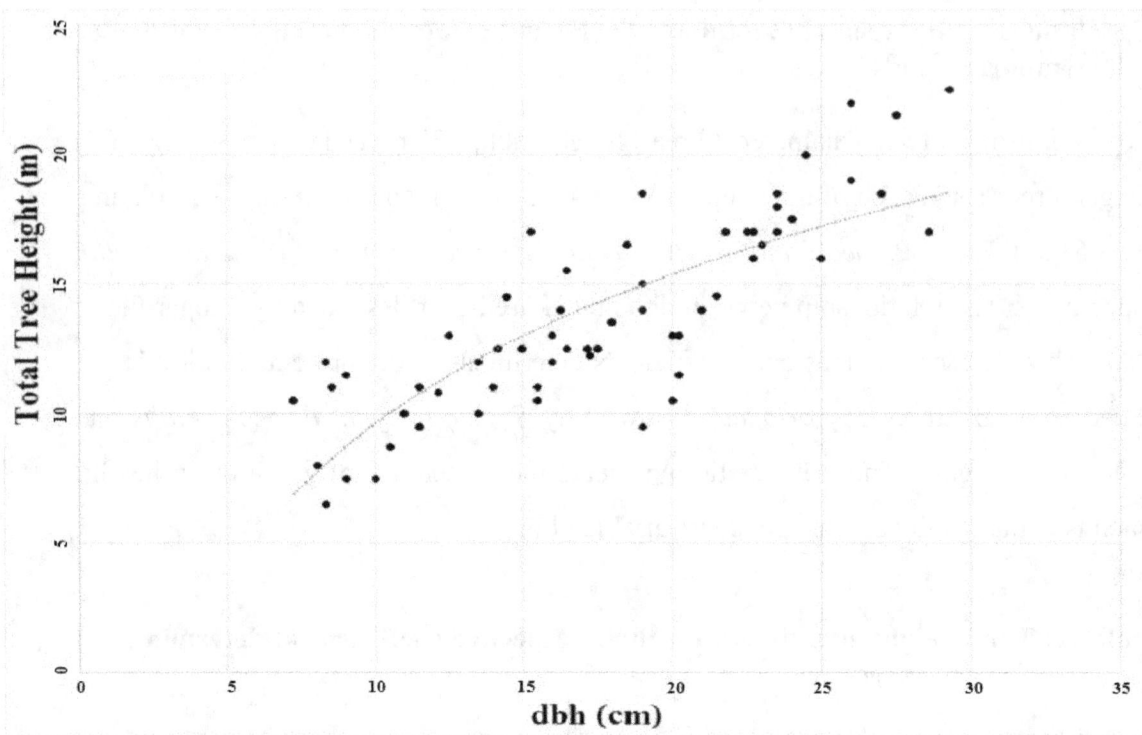

Figure 4. Relationship between diameter at breast height (dbh, 1.30 m) and total tree height (H) of signature trees in each of the temporary plots for *P. occidentalis*.

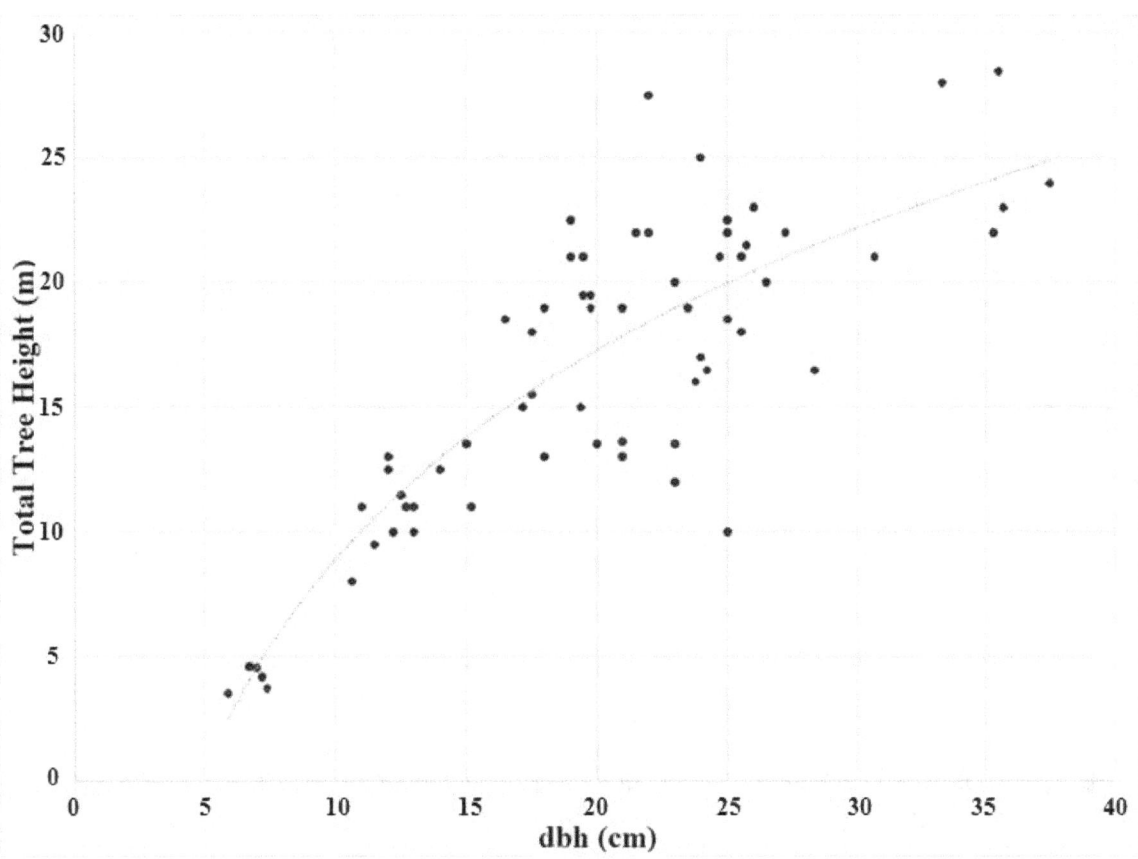

Figure 5. Relationship between diameter at breast height (dbh, 1.30 m) and total tree height (H) of signature trees in each of the temporary plots for *P. caribaea* var. Caribaea.

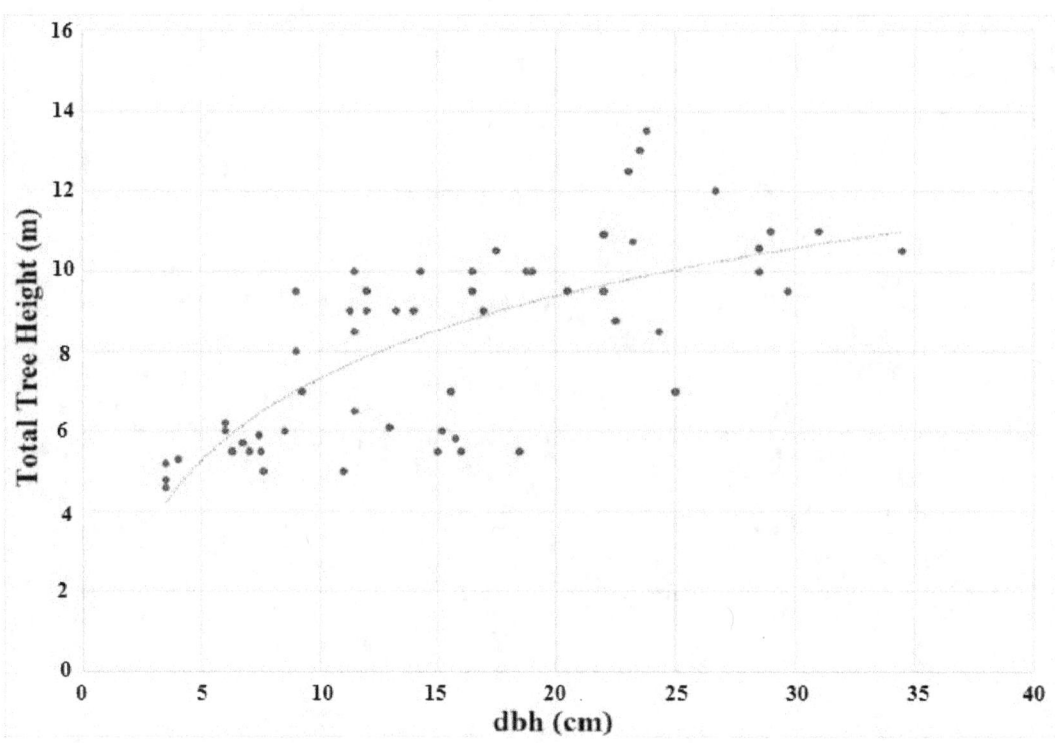

Figure 6. Relationship between diameter at breast height (dbh, 1.30 m) and total tree height (H) of signature trees in each of the temporary plots for *S. mahagoni.*

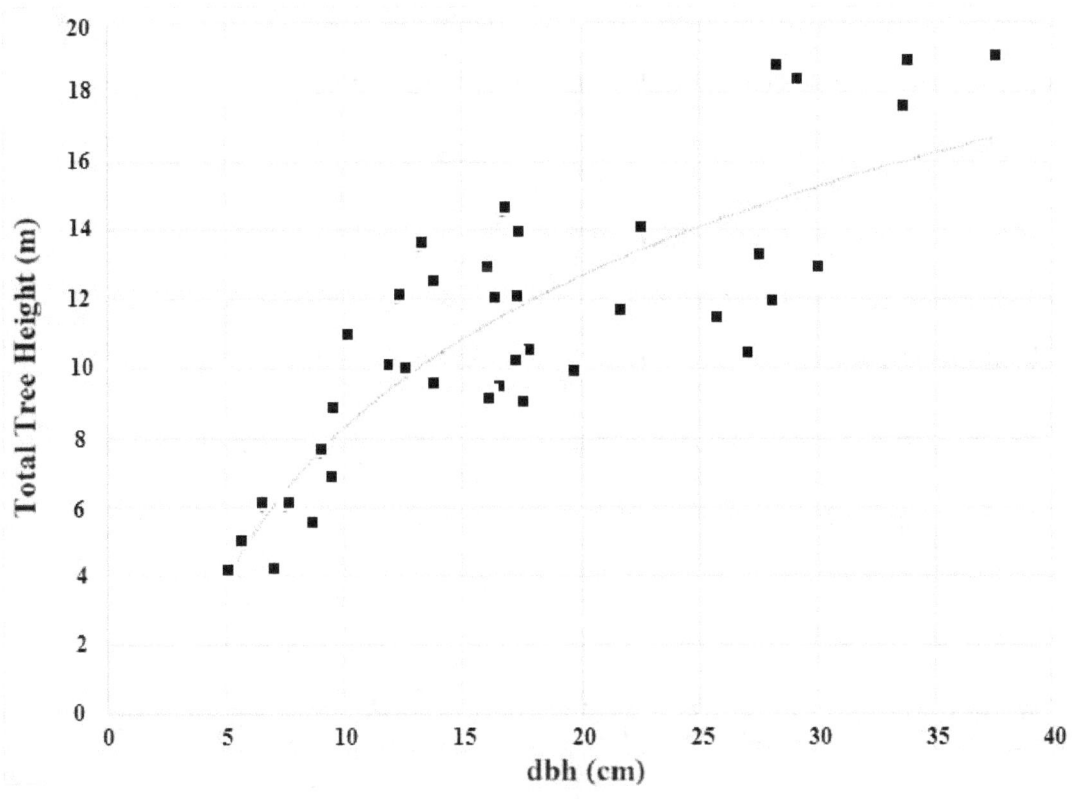

Figure 7. Relationship between diameter at breast height (dbh, 1.30 m) and total tree height (H) of signature trees in each of the temporary plots for *S. macrophylla*.

In terms of volume including bark, this is best estimated with the independent variable dbh^2H, for all species. Volume equations with their respective statistics for each species are presented in Table 13 along with their respective coefficient of determination (R2). The independent variable dbh^2H explains 97% of volume variability for *P. occidentalis* and *P. caribaea*; 90% for *S. mahagoni* and 96% for *S. macrophylla*.

Table 13. Volume equations and relevant statistics for each species.

Species	Parameter	Coefficients	R2	Standard Error of Estimation	t	Sig.
P. occidentalis	Intercept	0.0098	0.97	0.03193	0.682	0.507
	dbh^2H	0.00003629			19.871	<0.000
P. caribaea	Intercept	0.0026	0.97	0.05896	0.109	0.915
	dbh^2H	0.0000385			20.302	<0.000
S. mahagoni	Intercept	0.0115	0.90	0.03214	0.908	0.383
	dbh^2H	0.0000276			10.036	<0.000
S. macrophylla	Intercept	-1.0174	0.96	0.04588	-0.772	0.465
	dbh^2H	0.00004243			12.431	<0.000

3.4 Aerial Biomass, density and dry-weight-fresh-weight ratio in stem subsamples

The relationship between volume and density allows for the estimation of biomass in biological entities. If we multiply these two variables we can obtain dry biomass of a body, in our case, the biomass of the stem, which is essential to indirectly determine its carbon content. Stem subsamples on each evaluated tree were obtained at relative heights of 0.1, 0.5 and 0.8. out of total tree height. Dry-weight / fresh-weight ratio of these subsamples is another way to determine the biomass of tree tissues (stem, branches and leaves).

This method was used to compute the density of stem and branches in laboratory conditions. This ratio value multiplied by the full fresh weight of the corresponding tissue in each tree was used to determine dry biomass in the destructively sampled trees. Averaged density (specific gravity) values are shown in Table 14 for the sub-samples taken from the stem by species At the three relative heights specified. Units are in g/cm3. This unit has a direct correspondence if it is converted to tons per cubic meter (Ton/m3); i.e. 1 g/cm3 is equal to 1 ton/m3. In addition, dry-weight / fresh-weight (%) is included.

As it can be seen, average specific density decreases as tree relative height increases in the bole of softwoods (*P. occidentalis* and *P. caribaea*), contrary to what was observed in the mahoganies (*S. mahagoni* and *S. macrophylla*) where a defined pattern is not discernible. The ratio between dry-weight / fresh-weight presents the same pattern in conifers, while in the mahoganies the pattern is not monotonic.

Table 14. Average values of density (specific gravity) in g/cm3 for sub-samples taken from the stem by species at three specified relative heights, , and weight dry-weight / fresh-weight relationship.

Relative Height	*P. occidentalis*		*P. caribaea*		*S. mahagoni*		*S. macrophylla*	
	Density (g/cm3)	Dry-weight / Fresh-weight (%)	Density (g/cm3)	Dry-weight / Fresh-weight (%)	Density (g/cm3)	Dry-weight / Fresh-weight (%)	Density (g/cm3)	Dry-weight / Fresh-weight (%)
0.1	0.51	0.55	0.49	0.51	0.58	0.61	0.50	0.58
0.5	0.46	0.52	0.44	0.46	0.56	0.68	0.53	0.61
0.8	0.47	0.48	0.39	0.42	0.61	0.62	0.53	0.59

For branches and leaves, the average ratio between dry-weight / fresh-weight discriminating by relative height is shown in Table 15.

Table 15. Averaged relationship between dry-weight / fresh-weight for branches and leaves discriminating by relative height.

Relative Height	*P. occidentalis* Dry-weight/Fresh-weight (%)		*P. caribaea* Dry-weight/Fresh-weight (%)		*S. mahagoni* Dry-weight/Fresh-weight (%)		*S. macrophylla* Dry-weight/Fresh-weight (%)	
	Branches	Leaves	Branches	Leaves	Branches	Leaves	Branches	Leaves
0.1	0.51	0.47	0.57	0.47	0.54	0.44	0.54	0.44
0.5	0.48	0.47	0.47	0.55	0.53	0.48	0.53	0.48
0.8	0.46	0.48	0.42	0.46	0.51	0.47	0.51	0.47

3.5 Aerial Biomass and carbon percentage in stem, branches and leaves of sampled trees

Tables 16, 18, 20 and 22, present for each tree dbh and H, dry aerial biomass in the stem, branches and foliage; carbon percentage and corresponding carbon content. Carbon dioxide equivalent (CO_2-equicalente) content stored by each tree by age class is displayed in the last column. In addition, averages for each age class are presented in tables 17, 19, 21, and 23. In case of *P. occidentalis* it may be notice that the size of the sample trees by age class is not appropriate, since representative trees for age classes 6 and 7 had lower dimensions, contrary to expectations, and therefore carbon content is lower. It would be advisable to increase sample size in these age classes to correct this situation.

We were expecting to find an increase in biomass positively correlated to age, however, the "sampled" trees are not representative of all the variability in dimensionality terms for the different age classes. The amount of biomass accumulated and therefore carbon captured is directly proportional to tree size. In the case of *P. occidentalis*, a single tree was sampled in age class 7. This tree is below average in term of dimensions to the average of trees in class 6. Its dbh was 21 cm and a total height 14,65 m, while the average of these variables for age class 6 was 24.5 cm and 18.17 m respectively. In addition, the dimensions in class 5 were higher than class 6.

Table 16. Relevant variables and carbon content of tissues and totals in sampled trees for *P. occidentalis*.

Age-Tree	dbh	H	Avg. C % Stem	Avg. C % Branch	Avg. C % Foliage	C in Bole (kg)	C in Branch (kg)	C in Foliage (kg)	Total C in Tree (kg)	CO2 Equivalent (Kg)
7-1	10.50	11.50	32.26	46.99	48.93	7.57	1.18	2.40	11.15	40.93
7-2	12.10	10.80	35.80	48.41	47.82	12.66	2.71	4.05	19.42	71.25
10-1	16.50	12.80	50.36	48.75	50.24	30.38	5.87	10.14	46.39	170.24
1022	10.50	12.25	38.22	47.44	49.17	6.02	1.78	1.07	8.87	32.54
12-1	17.50	8.70	40.03	47.52	49.66	22.18	13.87	8.34	44.38	162.88
15-1	17.00	11.50	41.50	47.52	48.49	26.36	10.17	7.07	43.59	159.98
18-1	15.70	15.60	33.18	46.76	47.60	29.23	6.01	6.83	42.07	154.40
20-1	22.70	15.30	34.18	46.00	50.34	46.70	11.27	13.26	71.23	261.41
20-3	23.50	22.00	25.07	48.94	49.03	48.00	11.83	7.97	67.80	248.83
23-1	19.00	18.17	30.65	47.57	46.34	33.54	6.94	4.80	45.28	166.17
25-2	23.50	21.20	40.85	48.84	48.51	107.00	14.11	9.78	130.89	480.36
25-3	27.00	15.90	35.72	46.80	48.96	72.69	10.82	6.21	89.72	329.27
30-1	27.50	21.80	33.49	46.06	50.70	79.16	15.22	11.99	106.37	390.37
30-2	21.50	14.53	38.18	46.89	48.40	40.61	12.19	5.89	58.69	215.41
33-1	21.00	14.65	40.46	47.83	48.65	42.10	12.21	6.74	61.05	224.06

Table 17. Relevant variables and carbon content of tissues and totals averaged by age class for *P. occidentalis*.

Age Class	dbh	H	Avg. C % Stem	Avg. C % Branch	Avg. C % Foliage	C in Bole (kg)	C in Branch (kg)	C in Foliage (kg)	Total C in Tree (kg)	CO2 Equivalent (Kg)
2	12.40	11.84	39.16	47.90	49.04	14.16	2.88	4.42	21.45	78.74
3	17.25	10.10	40.76	47.52	49.07	24.27	12.02	7.70	43.99	161.43
4	20.63	17.63	30.81	47.23	48.99	41.31	9.70	9.36	60.37	221.55
5	23.17	18.42	35.74	47.74	47.93	71.08	10.62	6.93	88.63	325.27
6	24.50	18.17	35.83	46.47	49.55	59.88	13.71	8.94	82.53	302.89
7	21.00	14.65	40.46	47.83	48.65	42.10	12.21	6.74	61.05	224.06

Age Class: 1 (0 – 5 years); 2 (6 – 10 years); 3 (11 – 15 years); 4 (16 – 20 years); 5 (21 – 25 years); 6 (26 – 30 years). 7 (31 – 35 years).

Table 18. Relevant variables, dry biomass and carbon content of tissues and total for *P. caribaea*.

Age-Tree	dbh	H	Avg. C % Stem	Avg. C % Branch	Avg. C % Foliage	C in Bole (kg)	C in Branch (kg)	C in Foliage (kg)	Total C in Tree (kg)	CO2 Equivalent (Kg)
7-1	7.40	2.74	28.73	46.02	45.12	1.19	0.40	2.11	3.70	13.57
7-2	13.20	8.75	30.26	45.93	46.35	7.35	2.59	4.86	14.80	54.33
9-1	12.70	11.12	35.05	48.61	49.17	10.44	2.61	3.97	17.01	62.44
10-1	19.40	15.35	48.24	46.83	48.73	51.25	5.77	20.43	77.46	284.27
10-2	17.20	13.90	32.15	43.67	46.12	18.76	3.23	5.98	27.98	102.68
15-1	22.40	13.64	48.81	46.76	51.04	46.39	5.13	9.67	61.19	224.57
20-1	17.50	17.80	35.57	46.03	43.05	29.86	4.12	3.61	37.58	137.93
20-2	21.00	19.45	37.59	47.06	46.30	49.40	6.76	7.61	63.78	234.06
21-1	19.80	19.14	34.13	39.06	48.00	47.27	5.90	5.84	59.00	216.55
24-1	25.50	21.04	30.76	45.29	47.79	61.60	18.26	11.40	91.25	334.90
25-1	30.70	27.30	44.71	47.07	47.50	160.31	11.67	5.87	177.86	652.75
25-3	25.00	18.97	34.55	46.21	49.59	88.16	16.33	14.81	119.30	437.84
30-3	35.00	22.90	38.00	42.36	39.32	211.46	57.15	17.53	286.14	1050.15
32-1	23.10	21.10	41.11	46.84	45.59	100.00	11.21	8.28	119.49	438.52
32-2	27.00	22.95	38.40	46.75	49.56	141.97	18.81	18.52	179.30	658.03

Table 19. Relevant variables, dry biomass and carbon content of tissues and totals averaged by age class for *P. caribaea*.

Age Class	dbh	H	Avg. C % Stem	Avg. C % Branch	Avg. C % Foliage	C in Bole (kg)	C in Branch (kg)	C in Foliage (kg)	Total C in Tree (kg)	CO2 Equivalent (Kg)
1	7.40	2.74	28.73	46.02	45.12	1.19	0.40	2.11	3.70	13.57
2	15.63	12.28	36.43	46.26	47.59	21.95	3.55	8.81	34.31	125.93
3	22.40	13.64	48.81	46.76	51.04	46.39	5.13	9.67	61.19	224.57
4	19.25	18.63	36.58	46.55	44.67	39.63	5.44	5.61	50.68	185.99
5	25.25	21.61	36.04	44.41	48.22	89.34	13.04	9.48	111.86	410.51
6	35.00	22.90	38.00	42.36	39.32	211.46	57.15	17.53	286.14	1050.15
7	25.05	22.03	39.75	46.79	47.58	120.98	15.01	13.40	149.39	548.28

Age Class: 1 (0 – 5 years); 2 (6 – 10 years); 3 (11 – 15 years); 4 (16 – 20 years); 5 (21 – 25 years); 6 (26 – 30 years). 7 (31 – 35 years).

Table 20. Relevant variables, dry biomass and carbon content of tissues and total for S. mahagoni.

Age-Tree	dbh	H	Avg. C % Stem	Avg. C % Branch	Avg. C % Foliage	C in Bole (kg)	C in Branch (kg)	C in Foliage (kg)	Total C in Tree (kg)	CO2 Equivalent (Kg)
5-1	5.90	4.52	42.39	46.52	47.14	1.38	0.77	0.69	2.84	10.43
5-2	6.90	6.00	42.99	38.62	46.57	2.96	1.41	0.76	5.14	18.86
10-1	12.50	9.60	33.16	43.32	47.35	10.38	11.74	2.01	24.14	88.60
15-1	14.70	8.07	38.21	41.84	44.92	14.76	13.02	4.23	32.01	117.48
17-1	13.90	10.63	37.84	40.41	43.91	18.17	10.52	2.50	31.19	114.45
17-2	9.50	7.10	35.82	41.89	43.02	5.00	3.20	1.08	9.27	34.04
25-1	14.40	9.60	36.45	45.31	48.13	19.15	18.65	5.27	43.07	158.06
30-2	22.50	8.75	31.70	43.47	43.44	31.73	35.82	6.47	74.02	271.66
30-1	22.00	10.90	38.90	41.87	46.92	61.48	57.39	7.64	126.51	464.29
35-1	24.25	8.00	39.76	42.71	44.71	29.01	126.43	11.87	167.31	614.03
35-2	23.20	10.72	38.20	40.11	49.49	44.22	70.36	4.30	118.88	436.30
35-3	15.80	5.82	37.97	43.62	47.02	12.21	21.25	2.70	36.16	132.70
35-4	34.50	10.55	33.41	42.48	45.95	63.14	79.58	14.77	157.49	577.98

Table 21. Relevant variables, dry biomass and carbon content of tissues and totals averaged by age class for *S. mahagoni*.

Age Class	dbh	H	Avg. C % Stem	Avg. C % Branch	Avg. C % Foliage	C in Bole (kg)	C in Branch (kg)	C in Foliage (kg)	Total C in Tree (kg)	CO_2 Equivalent (Kg)
1	5.90	4.52	42.39	46.52	47.14	1.38	0.77	0.69	2.84	10.43
2	6.90	6.00	42.99	38.62	46.57	2.96	1.41	0.76	5.14	18.86
3	13.60	8.84	35.69	42.58	46.14	12.57	12.38	3.12	28.08	103.04
4	11.70	8.87	36.83	41.15	43.46	11.59	6.86	1.79	20.23	74.24
5	14.40	9.60	36.45	45.31	48.13	19.15	18.65	5.27	43.07	158.06
6	22.50	8.75	31.70	43.47	43.44	31.73	35.82	6.47	74.02	271.66
7	23.95	9.20	37.65	42.16	46.82	42.01	71.00	8.26	121.27	445.06

Age Class: 1 (0 – 5 years); 2 (6 – 10 years); 3 (11 – 15 years); 4 (16 – 20 years); 5 (21 – 25 years); 6 (26 – 30 years). 7 (31 – 35 years).

Table 22. Relevant variables, dry biomass and carbon content of tissues and total for *S. macrophylla*.

Age-Tree	dbh	H	Avg. C % Stem	Avg. C % Branch	Avg. C % Foliage	C in Bole (kg)	C in Branch (kg)	C in Foliage (kg)	Total C in Tree (kg)	CO2 Equivalent (Kg)
5-1	7.6	4.6	39.46	42.21	44.17	2.23	0.60	0.46	3.28	12.05
5-2	9.5	8.8	35.14	42.87	44.05	5.30	2.08	4.51	11.89	43.64
10-2	17.3	10.3	31.4	43.14	43.96	18.56	25.63	7.51	51.70	189.75
10-1	21.6	11.7	39.6	38.29	44.26	35.15	26.41	5.30	66.87	245.40
15-3	14	13.15	34.14	41.52	47.47	23.88	10.30	3.15	37.33	136.98
17-1	14.7	11.5	40.60	42.37	44.32	19.93	13.41	2.45	35.79	131.35
18-1	16.9	14.2	40.73	38.75	42.44	29.14	8.06	4.54	41.74	153.18
20-1	28.2	18.75	36.66	42.06	42.84	48.49	16.51	93.19	158.20	580.58
20-2	27.5	13.3	33.43	42.47	43.72	55.35	74.58	14.00	143.93	528.22

Table 23. Relevant variables, dry biomass and carbon content of tissues and totals averaged by age class for *S. macrophylla*.

Age Class	dbh	H	Avg. C % Stem	Avg. C % Branch	Avg. C % Foliage	C in Bole (kg)	C in Branch (kg)	C in Foliage (kg)	Total C in Tree (kg)	CO2 Equivalent (Kg)
1	8.55	6.70	37.30	42.54	44.11	3.76	1.34	2.49	7.59	27.85
2	17.30	10.30	31.40	43.14	43.96	18.56	25.63	7.51	51.70	189.75
3	17.80	12.43	36.87	39.91	45.87	29.52	18.35	4.23	52.10	191.20
4	21.83	14.44	37.86	41.41	43.33	38.23	28.14	28.55	94.91	348.34

Age Class: 1 (0 – 5 years); 2 (6 – 10 years); 3 (11 – 15 years); 4 (16 – 20 years); 5 (21 – 25 years); 6 (26 – 30 years). 7 (31 – 35 years).

For *P. caribaea*, it was found that the tree representative of class 6 is approximately two times greater than the two trees sampled in class 7. In S. mahagoni, two trees in class 4 have inferior dimensions on average than those of the class 3. The situation in *S. macrophylla* follows the desired pattern. For the study to be logical, it is necessary to increase the number of trees sampled in problematic age classes. The selection of representative trees in each class should be random, and with a similar amount of trees in each class.

The next graphs (Figures 8, 9, and 10) show for each species, averages of total dry aerial biomass and carbon concentration in tissues, as well as carbon dioxide equivalent (CO2_equivalente) captured. On average, the greater amount of dry biomass is contain in *P. caribaea*, followed by *P. occidentalis*. The least amount of dry aerial biomass was found in S. mahagoni. Average concentration of carbon in the stem was higher for *P. caribaea*, closely followed by *S. mahogany*, *P. occidentalis* and finally *S. macrophylla*. *P. occidentalis* has higher concentrations of carbon in leaves and branches to other species.

In regards to carbon content, derived by multiplying the dry biomass by concentration of carbon, *P. caribaea* turned out to be the species with higher content and therefore its capture of CO2 equivalent is higher on average (365.81 kg). An analysis of variance (Table 24) shows that the concentration of carbon in the branches is statistically significant and greater in *P. occidentalis* than in both mahogany species. Further more, the concentration of carbon in the branches of *P. caribaea* is statistically significant and larger than in *S. macrophylla*. Foliage of *P. occidentalis* has one higher concentration of carbon in the foliage than the counterpart in *S. macrophylla*.

Table 24. Results of the analysis of variance in regards to carbon concentration in different tissues and species.

Test: Bonferroni						95% Confidence Interval	
Tissue	(I) Specie	(J) Specie	Mean Difference (I-J)	Std. Error	Sig.	Lower Bound	Upper Bound
Branches	occidentalis	mahagoni	4.619*	1.02	0.00	1.64	7.60
		macrophylla	5.701*	1.18	0.00	2.24	9.16
	caribaea	macrophylla	3.850*	1.15	0.02	0.49	7.21
Foliage	occidentalis	macrophylla	4.556*	1.48	0.04	0.22	8.89

Discriminating by age, the behavior of carbon dioxide equivalent (CO_2-equivalent) in the trees sampled is presented in Figure 11 for *P. occidentalis, P. caribaea, S. mahagoni* and *S. macrophylla*.

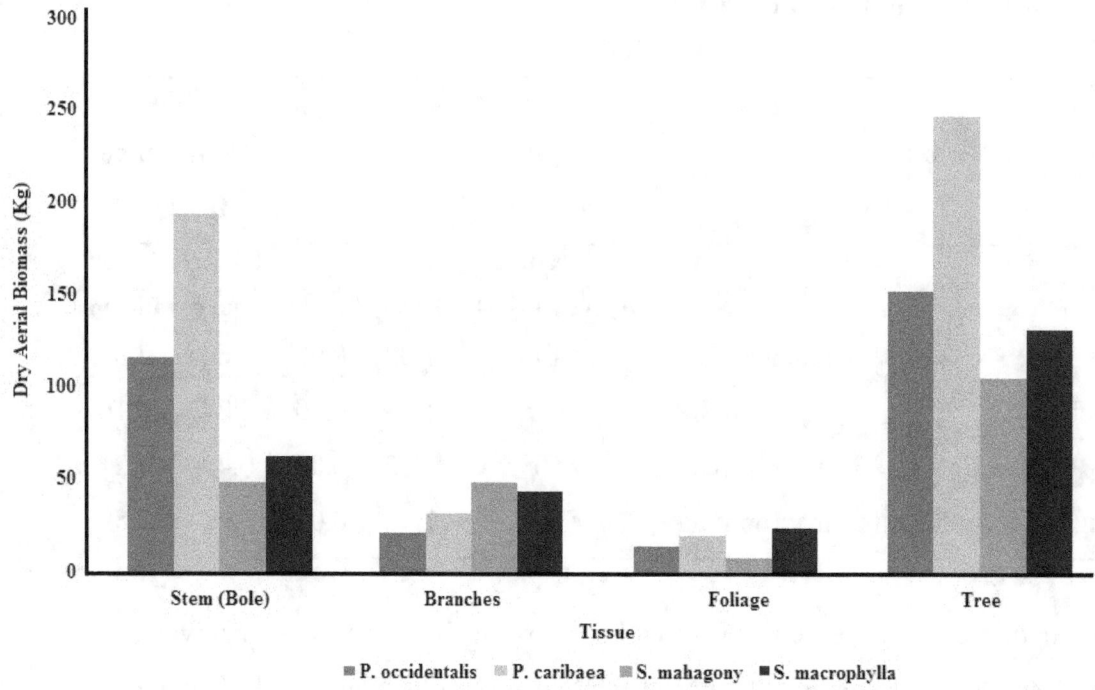

Figure 8. Average dry aerial biomass for all ages in tissues by species.

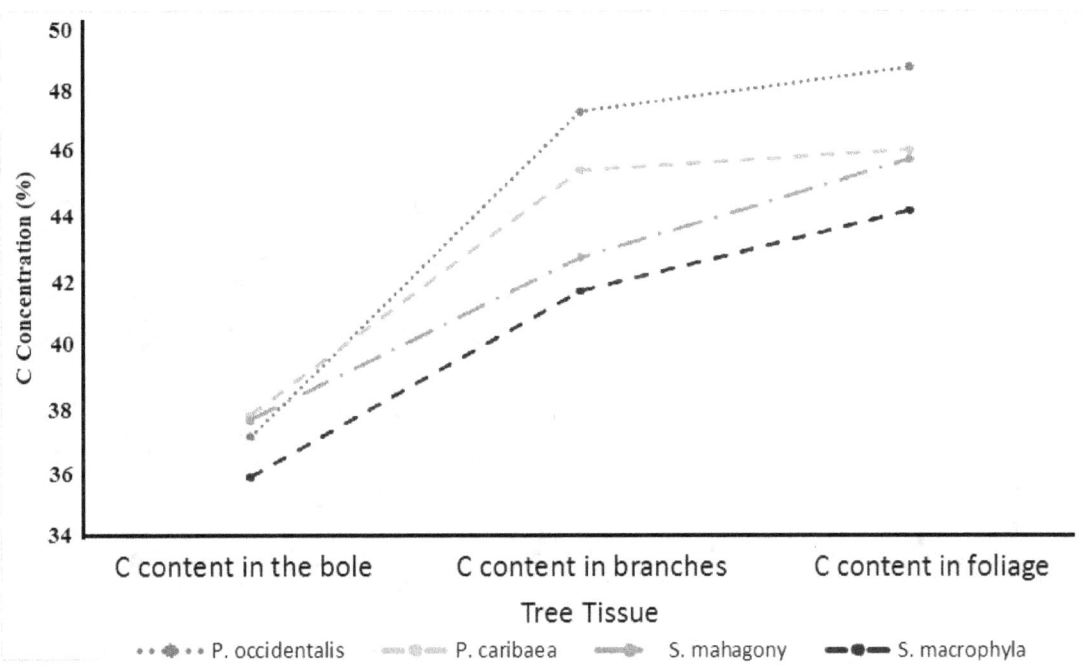

Figure 9. Average concentration of carbon for all ages in tissues by species.

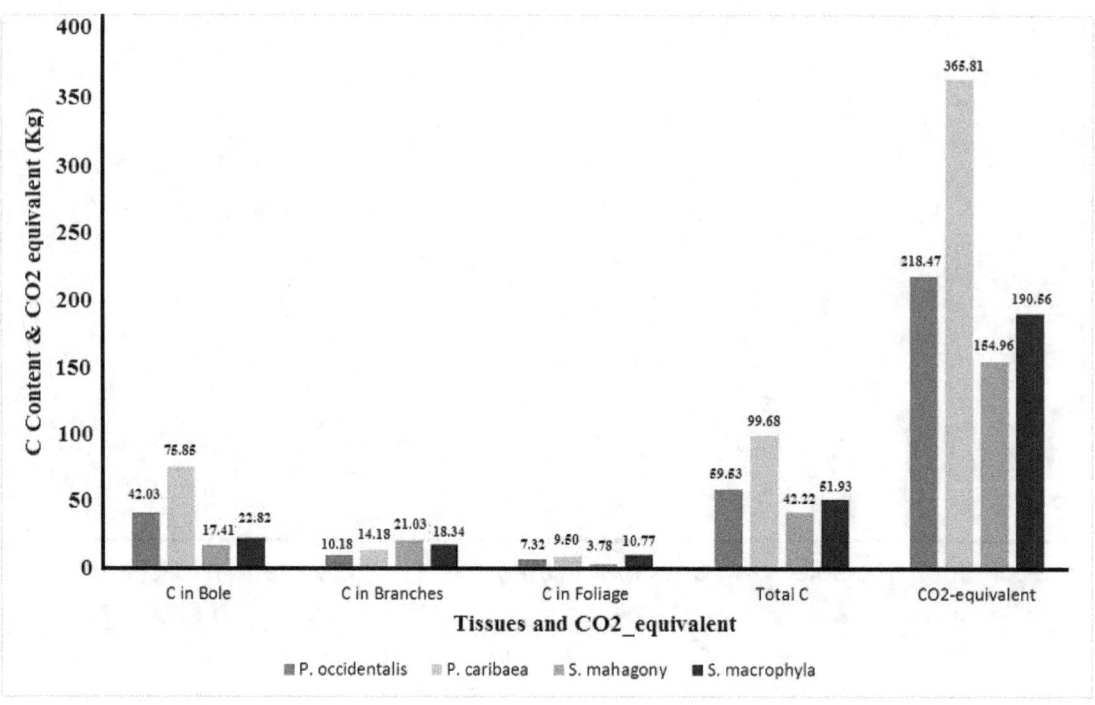

Figure 10. C content and CO2_equivalent average for all ages in tissues by species.

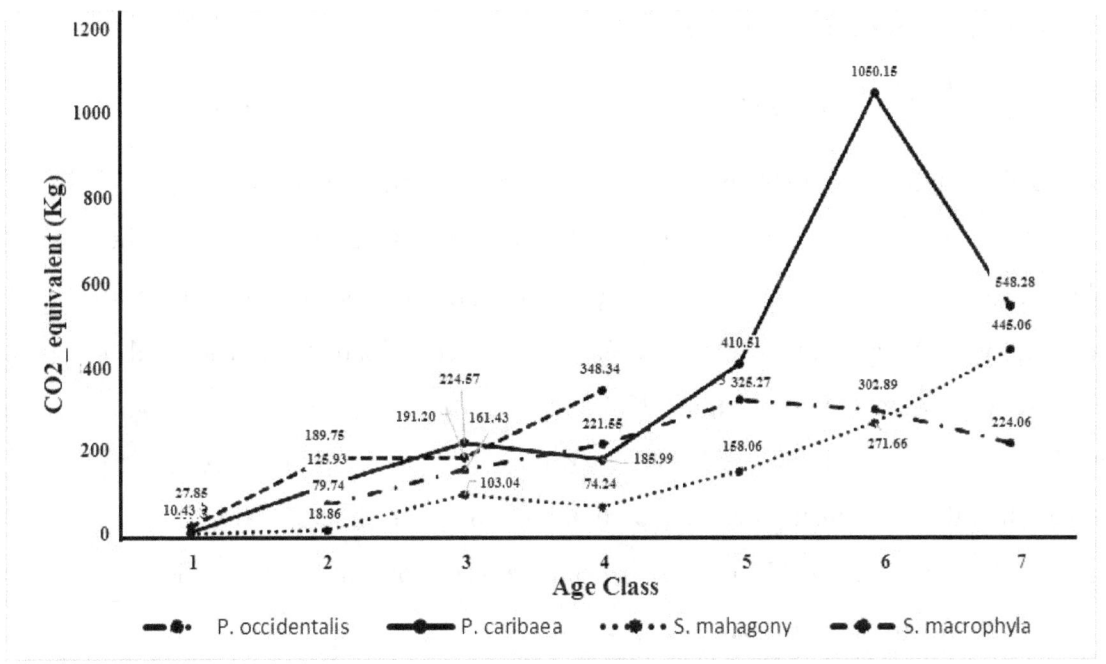

Figure 11. CO2_equivalent of sampled trees for each species according to age class.

3.6 Allometric equations development

3.6.1 Exploration of the relationship between dependent and independent variable

To explore the relationship between aerial total carbon content and the independent variables dbh and dbh^2H, carbon content (TC) data points were plotted against these variables. The combined variable dbh^2H is an approximation of the volume of the trunk (considering form factor) and it can therefore be used as a combined effect. The resulting scatterplot diagrams are shown in Figure 12 (*P. occidentalis*); Figure 13 (*P. caribaea*). Figure 14 (*S. mahagoni*); and Figure 15 (*S. macrophylla*). Observing the plots, it can be clearly seen that the relationship between carbon and dbh is not linear, and variation of carbon content increases with dbh. The relationship between carbon and dbh^2H is linear, but the variation of carbon increases.

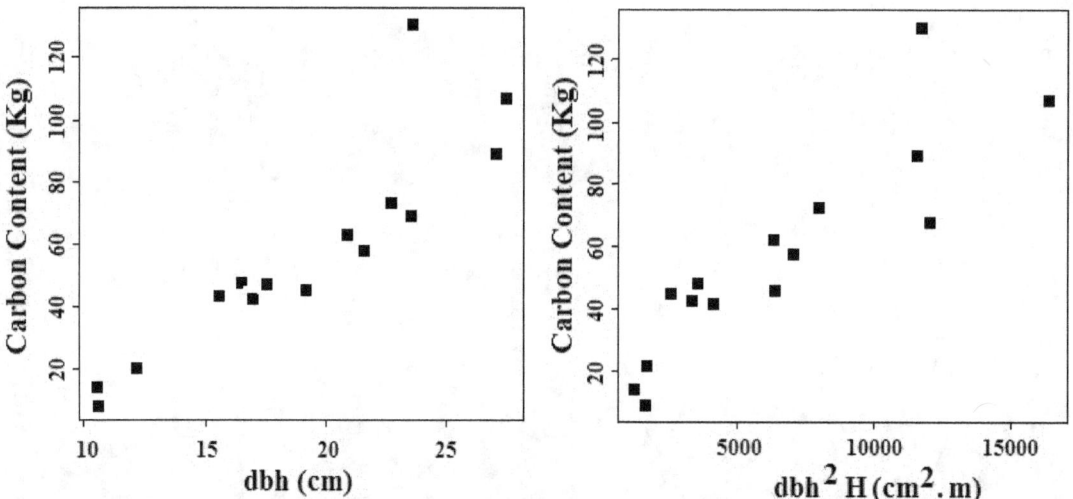

Figure 12. Relationship between total carbon and the independent variables dbh and dbh2H for *P. occidentalis*.

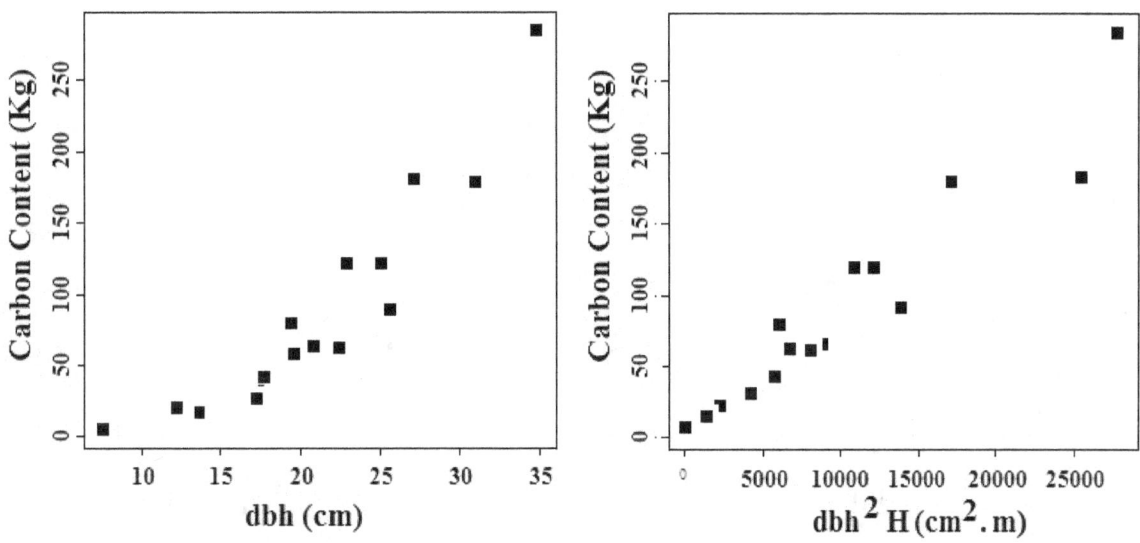

Figure 13. Relationship between total carbon and the independent variables dbh and dbh2H for *P. caribaea*.

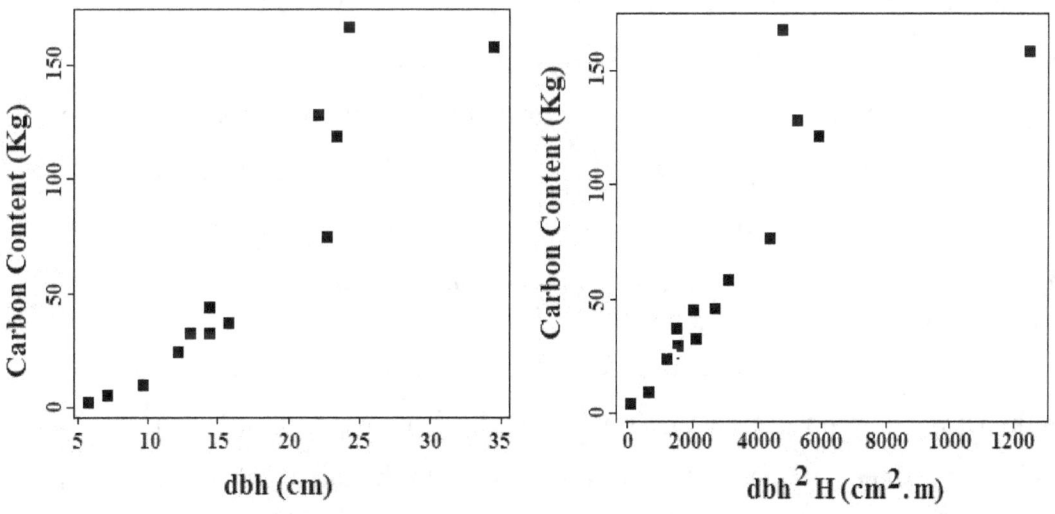

Figure 14. Relationship between total carbon and the independent variables dbh and dbh2H for *S. mahagoni*.

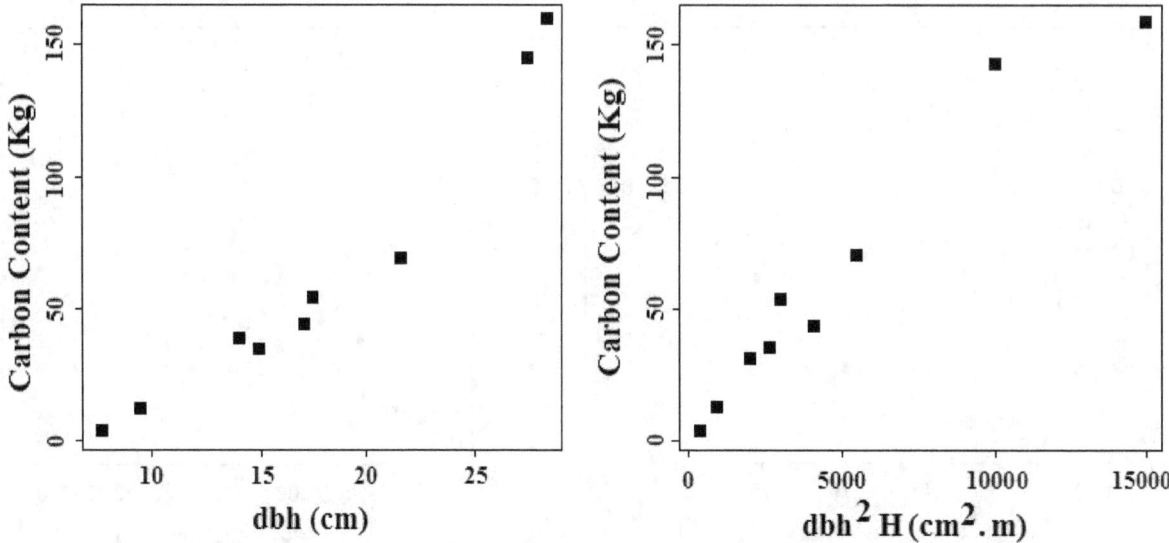

Figure 15. Relationship between total carbon and the independent variables dbh and dbh2H for *S. macrophylla*.

When the relationship between the dependent and independent variables is not linear, or when the variance increases with the increase of the independent variable, as it is natural in the biological variables, it is possible to use logarithmic transformations in one or both types of variables. A simultaneous logarithmic transformation in both, independent and dependent variables was employed to see how they behaved. The resulting scatterplot diagrams after transformation are shown in Figure 16 (*P. occidentalis*); Figure 17 (*P. caribaea*). Figure 18 (*S. mahagoni*); and Figure 19 (*S. macrophylla*).

For the first case, the logarithmic transformation in both variables has made the relationship between carbon and dbh linear: the relationship between ln (dbh) and ln (TC) is a straight line and the variance of TC does not vary with the diameter. In the second case, the logarithmic transformation for the relationship between ln (dbh2H) and ln (TC) is a straight line and the variance of TC does not vary as the independent variable increases.

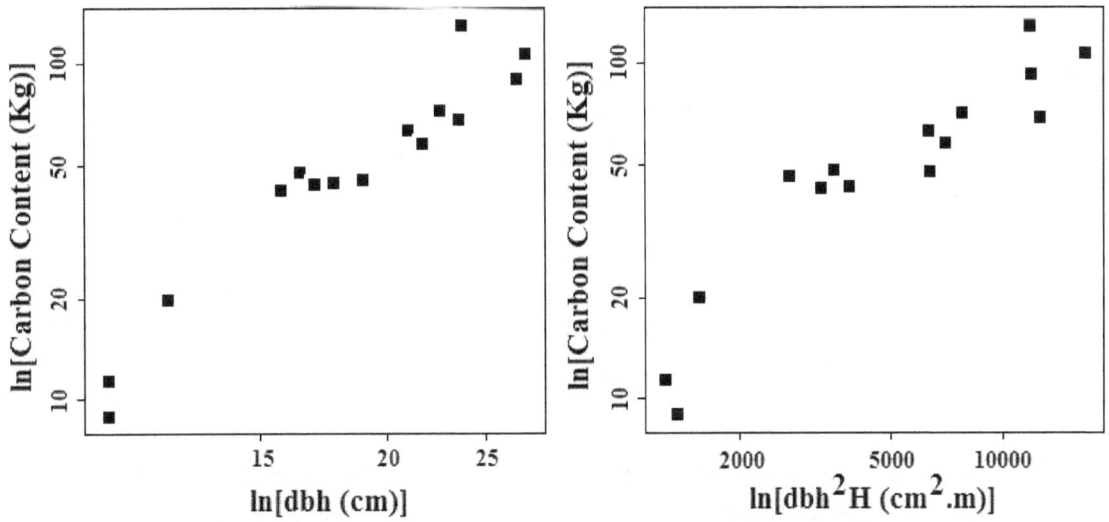

Figure 16. Relationship between the natural logarithm of total carbon and the natural logarithm of the independent variables dbh and dbh2H for *P. occidentalis*.

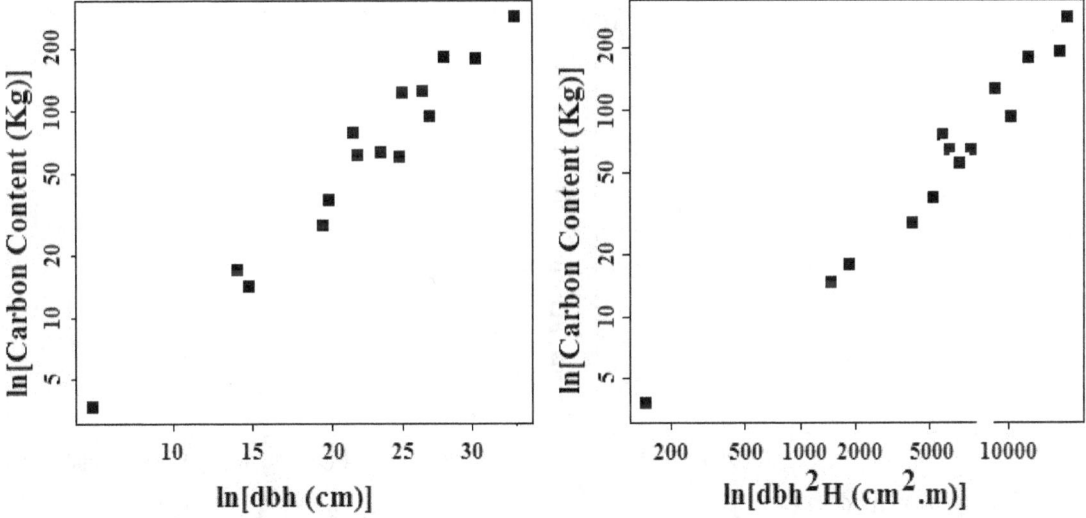

Figure 17. Relationship between the natural logarithm of total carbon and the natural logarithm of the independent variables dbh and dbh2H for *P. caribaea*.

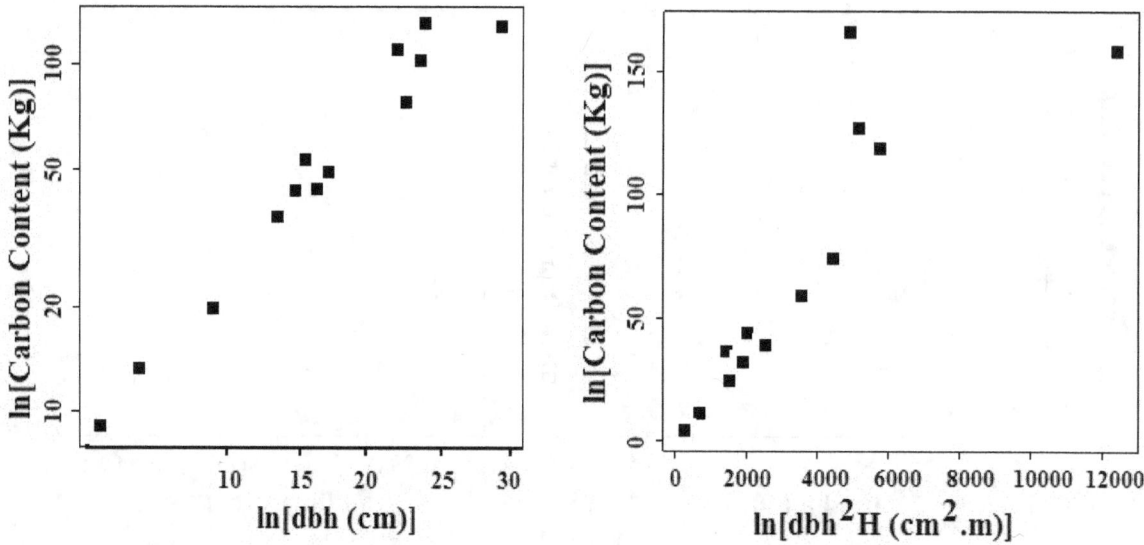

Figure 18. Relationship between the natural logarithm of total carbon and the natural logarithm of the independent variables dbh and dbh2H for *S. mahagoni.*

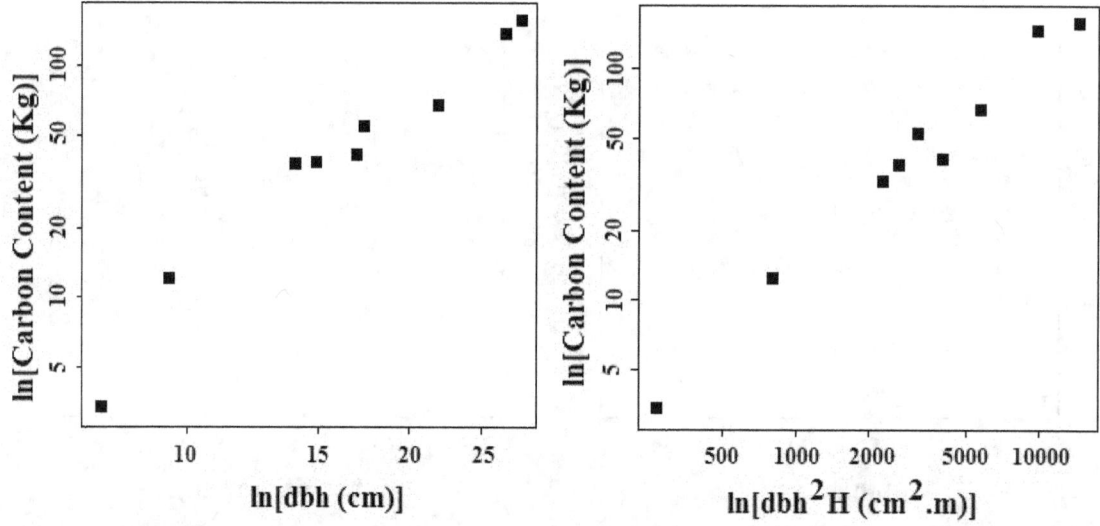

Figure 19. Relationship between the natural logarithm of total carbon and the natural logarithm of the independent variables dbh and dbh2H for *S. macrophylla.*
3.6.2 Lineal regression between ln (TC) and ln (dbh)

The exploratory analysis (Figure 16) showed that the relationship between the natural logarithm of total carbon content and the natural logarithm of the variables dbh and dbh2H was linear for all species, with a variation in TC, which was approximately constant. A simple linear regression to predict ln (TC) from ln (dbh) by modeling $ln(TC) = b_0 + b_1 ln(dbh) + \varepsilon$, where Var $(\varepsilon) = \sigma^2$ should be appropriate, using the method of ordinary least squares. The parameterization of the resulting equations *for P. occidentalis, P. caribaea, S. mahagoni* and S. *macrophylla* is shown below (Table 25).

Table 25. Coefficients and corresponding statistics for the fitting of the data using simple linear regression between ln (TC) and ln (dbh) to estimate aerial carbon content on *P. occidentalis, P. caribaea, S. mahagoni* and *S. macrophylla*.

Species	Parameters	Coefficients	Standard Error	t	Pr(>|t|)	AIC
P. occidentalis	Intercept	-3.009	0.561	-5.364	<0.000	1.613
	log(dbh)	2.35	0.192	12.228	<0.000	
P. caribaea	Intercept	-4.498	0.443	-10.161	<0.000	0.308
	log(dbh)	2.858	0.147	19.454	<0.000	
S. mahagoni	Intercept	-3.186	0.432	-7.383	<0.000	7.394
	log(dbh)	2.488	0.156	15.918	<0.000	
S. macrophylla	Intercept	-3.755	0.5975	-6.285	<0.000	5.439
	log(dbh)	2.661	0.2126	12.518	<0.000	

For all four species, the coefficients for intercept and slope are statistically significant (P-value < 0.05). In *P. occidentalis* the standard error of residuals is 0.2246 with 13 degrees of freedom (df), the coefficient of multiple determination (R2) is 0.92, and the F statistic is 149.5 with 1 and 13 df. In *P. caribaea*, the standard error of residuals is 0.215 with 13 df; R2 is 0.97, and the F statistic is 378.1 with 1 and 13 df. For S. mahagoni, the corresponding statistics values are, 0.277 with 11 df, R2 is 0.96, and the F statistic is 253.4 with 1 and 11 df. In the case of *S. macrophylla*, the standard error of the residuals is 0.266 with 7 df, R2 is 0.96, and the F statistic is 156.7 with 1 and 7 df. Logarithmic equations and their respective transformations using the inverse function of exponentiation are presented in Table 26.

Table 26. Logarithmic equations and their respective transformations using the inverse function of exponentiation obtained for each species by simple linear regression of the dependent variable TC and the independent dbh.

Species	Logarithmic Equation	Model	Exponential Transformation **	Model
P. occidentalis	$ln(TC)$ $= -3.0096 + 2.3504\,ln(dbh)$	[1]	$TC = 0.0493\,(dbh)^{2.3504}$	[1.1]
P. caribaea	$ln(TC)$ $= -4.498 + 2.8581\,ln(dbh)$	[4]	$TC = 0.0111\,(dbh)^{2.8581}$	[4.1]
S. mahagoni	$ln(TC)$ $= -3.1864 + 2.4887\,ln(dbh)$	[6]	$TC = 0.0413\,(dbh)^{2.4887}$	[6.1]
S. macrophylla	$ln(TC)$ $= -3.7555 + 2.6619\,ln(dbh)$	[8]	TC $= 0.02339\,(dbh)^{2.6619}$	[8.1]

** Allows for estimations in original scale of the data.

To corroborate graphically that the hypothesis for linear regression are satisfied, graphic tools such as Quantile-Quantile plots for "Normal Distribution" and the diagram of dispersion of residuals versus the fitted values for each of the species were used and are displayed in Figures 20, 21, 22 and 23.

For *P. occidentalis*, the quantile - quantile plot presents the expected pattern while the residuals versus the fitted values plot indicate the presence of bias. For *P. caribaea* the quantile - quantile plot seems to have a light structure. The residuals versus fitted values plot shows a random pattern of dispersion, much better than the corresponding plot for *P. occidentalis*. The quantile- quantile plot for S. mahagoni also shows slight deviation to what was expected in the first observations, and the residuals versus fitted values show a pattern of uneven dispersion around the residual value 0. In the case of *S. macrophylla*, the QQ presents a proper dispersion except the first observation. The presence of bias in the graph of residuals versus fitted values is noticeable. It can be assumed that the hypothesis for simple linear regression are met in a range that goes from poorly to moderately fashion. The small sample size may be the main cause of this behavior.

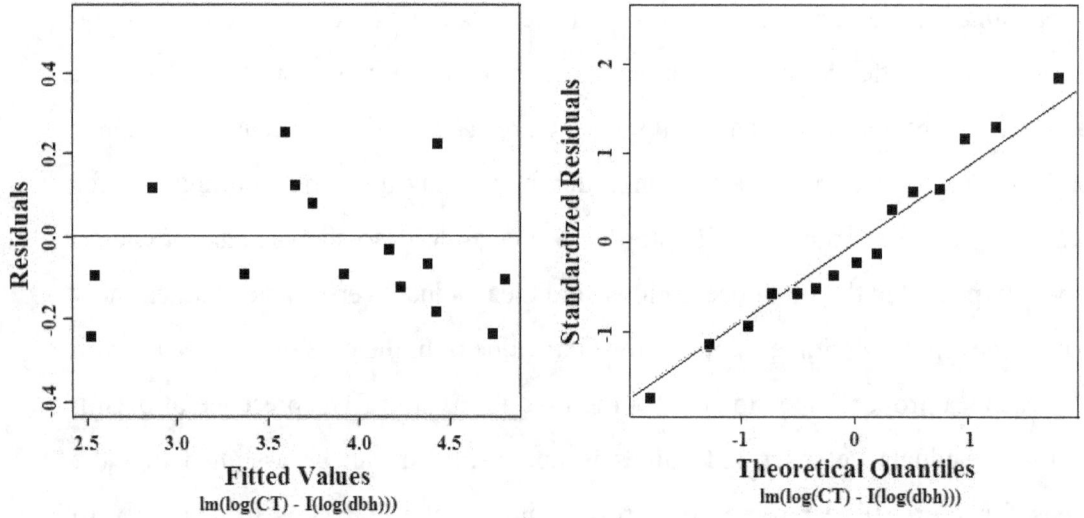

Figure 20. Residuals plotted against fitted values (left) and diagram quantile - quantile (right) for simple linear regression ln (TC) against ln (dbh) applied to the species *P. occidentalis*.

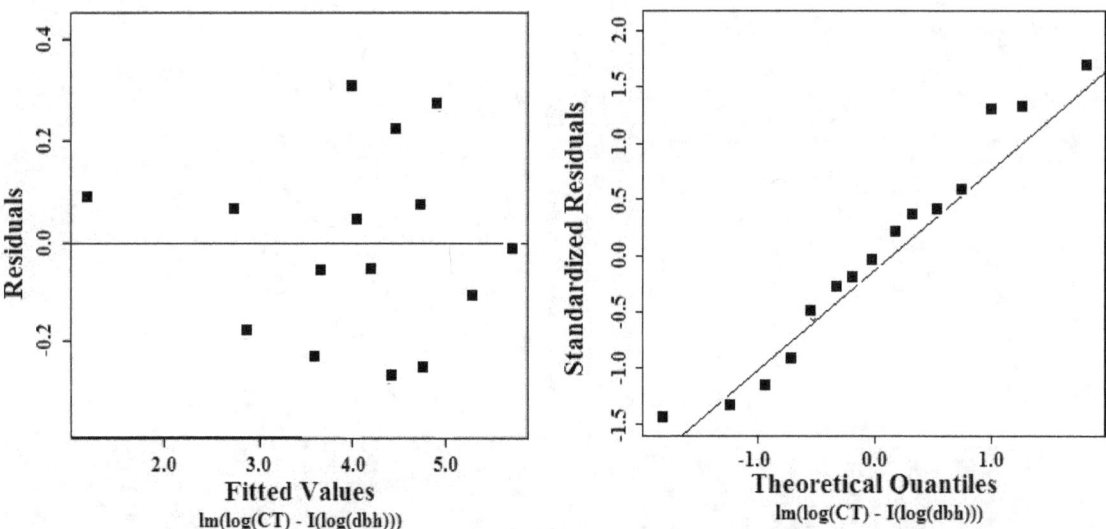

Figure 21. Residuals plotted against fitted values (left) and diagram quantile - quantile (right) for simple linear regression ln (TC) against ln (dbh) applied to the species *P. caribaea* var Caribaea.

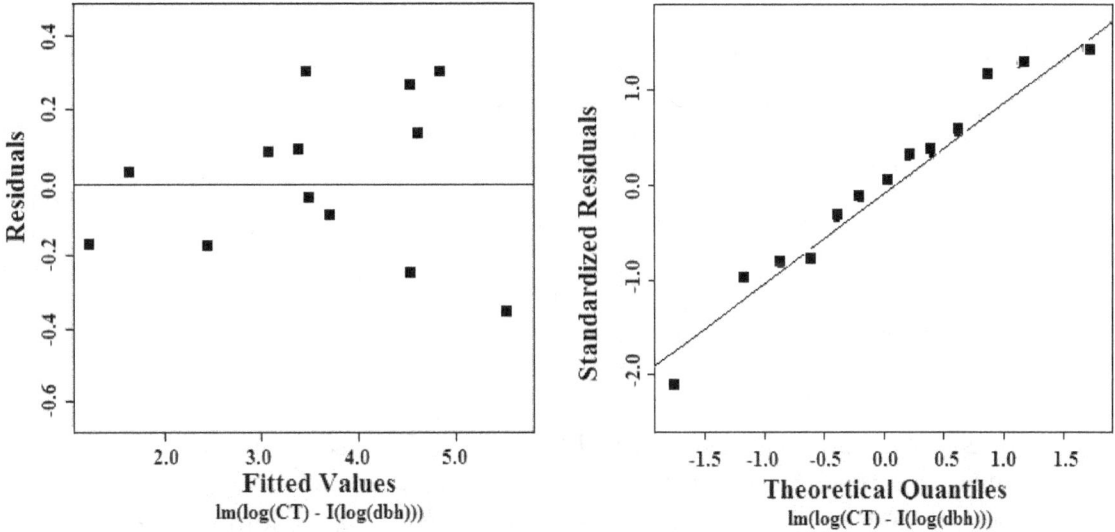

Figure 22. Residuals plotted against fitted values (left) and diagram quantile - quantile (right) for simple linear regression ln (TC) against ln (dbh) applied to the species *S. mahagoni*.

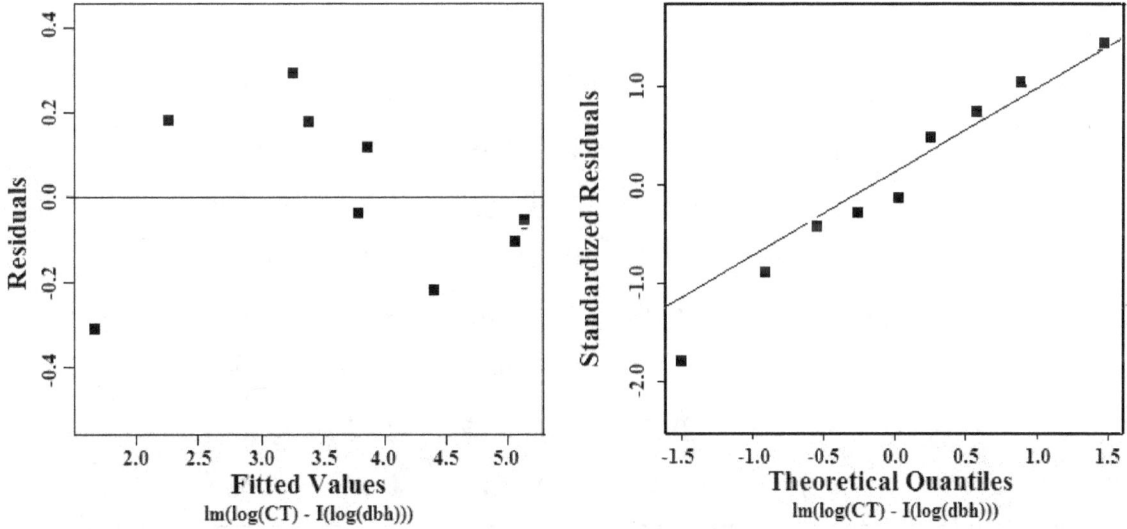

Figure 23. Residuals plotted against fitted values (left) and diagram quantile - quantile (right) for simple linear regression ln (TC) against ln (dbh) applied to the species *S. macrophylla*.

3.6.3 Simple lineal regression between ln (TC) y ln (dbh²H)

Earlier exploratory analysis (Figure 17) showed that the relationship between the natural logarithm of total carbon content and the natural logarithm of DAP^2H was linear, with a variation of TC, which was approximately constant. Therefore, a simple linear regression to predict ln (TC) from ln (dbh^2H) of the form: $ln(TC) = b_0 + b_1 ln(dbh^2H) + \varepsilon$, where Var $(\varepsilon) = \sigma^2$ would be also suitable. The regression is adjusted using the method of ordinary least squares. The parameterization of the resulting equations for four evaluated species is shown in Table 27.

Table 27. Coefficients and corresponding fit statistics for the data using simple lineal regression between ln (TC) and ln ((dbh^2H) for estimating aerial carbon content in *P. occidentalis, P. caribaea, S. mahagoni* and *S. macrophylla*.

Species	Parameters	Coefficients	Standard Error	t	Pr(>|t|)	AIC
P. occidentalis	Intercept	-3.401	0.813	-4.185	<0.000	10.058
	$log(dbh^2H)$	0.850	0.095	8.919	<0.000	
P. caribaea	Intercept	-3.255	0.485	-6.716	<0.000	7.363
	$log(dbh^2H)$	0.838	0.055	15.211	<0.000	
S. mahagoni	Intercept	-4.1618	0.5013	-8.303	<0.000	7.859
	$log(dbh^2H)$	1.0263	0.0657	15.623	<0.000	
S. macrophylla	Intercept	-4.0609	0.3922	-10.36	<0.000	-2.624
	$log(dbh^2H)$	0.9668	0.04871	19.85	<0.000	

Intercept and slope coefficients are statistically significant (P-value < 0.05) for the equations of all species. The equation of *P. occidentalis* has a residual standard error of 0.298 with 13 degrees of freedom (df), the coefficient of multiple determination (R^2) is 0.86, and the F statistic is 79.5 with 1 and 13 df. In *P. caribaea*, the residual standard error is 0.272 with 13 df, R^2 is 0.95, and the F statistic is 231.4 with 1 and 13 df. For S. mahagoni, the standard error of the residuals is 0.283 with 11 df, R^2 is 0.96, and the F statistic is 244.1 with gl 1 and 11 df. Finally, for *S. macrophylla*, the standard error of the residuals is 0.169 with 7 df, R^2 is 0.98, and the F statistic is 394.1 with 1 and 7 df.

Logarithmic equations and their respective transformations using the inverse function of exponentiation obtained for each species and using simple linear regression of the independent and the dependent variable TC and independent variable ($dbh^2 H$) are presented below Table 28.

Table 28. Logarithmic equations and their respective transformations using the inverse function of exponentiation, obtained for each species using simple linear regression of the dependent variable TC and the independent dbh^2H.

Species	Logarithmic Equation	Model	Exponential Transformation **	Model
P. occidentalis	$ln(TC)$ = −3.401 + 0.8501 $ln(dbh^2H)$	[2]	$TC = 0.033\,(dbh^2H)^{0.8501}$	[2.1]
P. caribaea	$ln(TC)$ = −3.2552 + 0.8379 $ln(dbh^2H)$	[5]	$TC = 0.039(dbh^2H)^{0.8379}$	[5.1]
S. mahagoni	$ln(TC)$ = −4.1618 + 1.0263 $ln(dbh^2H)$	[7]	$TC = 0.016\,(dbh^2H)^{1.0263}$	[7.1]
S. macrophylla	$ln(TC)$ = −4.0609 + 0.9668 $ln(dbh^2H)$	[9]	$TC = 0.017\,(dbh^2H)^{0.9668}$	[9.1]

** Allows for estimations in original scale of the data.

Graphic verification of lineal regression hypotheses, namely scatterplots of residuals versus fitted values (left) and Quantile-Quantile plots (right) and are presented in Figures 24, 25, 26 and 27. Quantile-Quantile plots show the expected ideal pattern and residuals versus the fitted values indicate the presence of bias in all cases. We argue that this situation arises naturally when working with different age classes and when the sample is too small. It can be assumed that the hypothesis of simple linear regression are met from in a poorly to moderately manner. In addition, regression coefficients are robust to deviations from assumptions of normality.

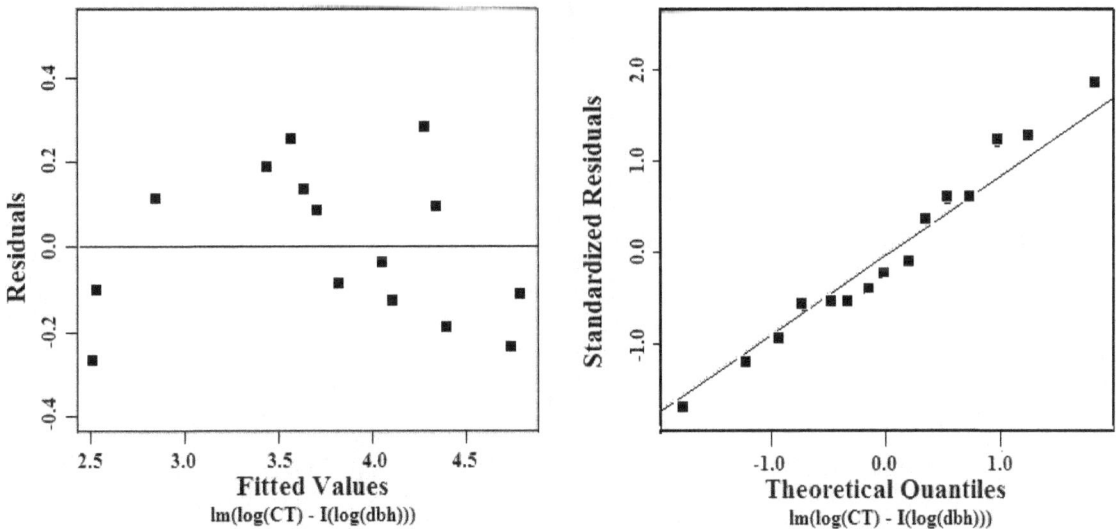

Figure 24. Residuals plotted against fitted values (left panels) and diagram quantile-quantile (right panels) for simple linear regression ln (TC) against ln (dbh2H) applied to the species *P. occidentalis*, in plantations established in La Sierra.

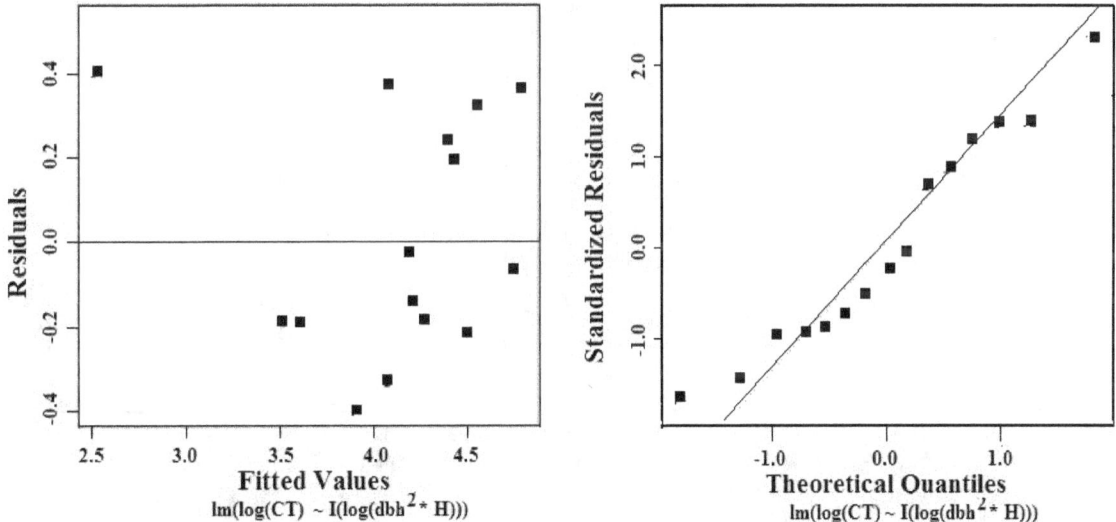

Figure 25. Residuals plotted against fitted values (left) and quantile - quantile diagram (right) for simple linear regression ln (TC) against ln (dbh2H) applied to the species *P. caribaea* var Caribaea, in plantations established in La Sierra.

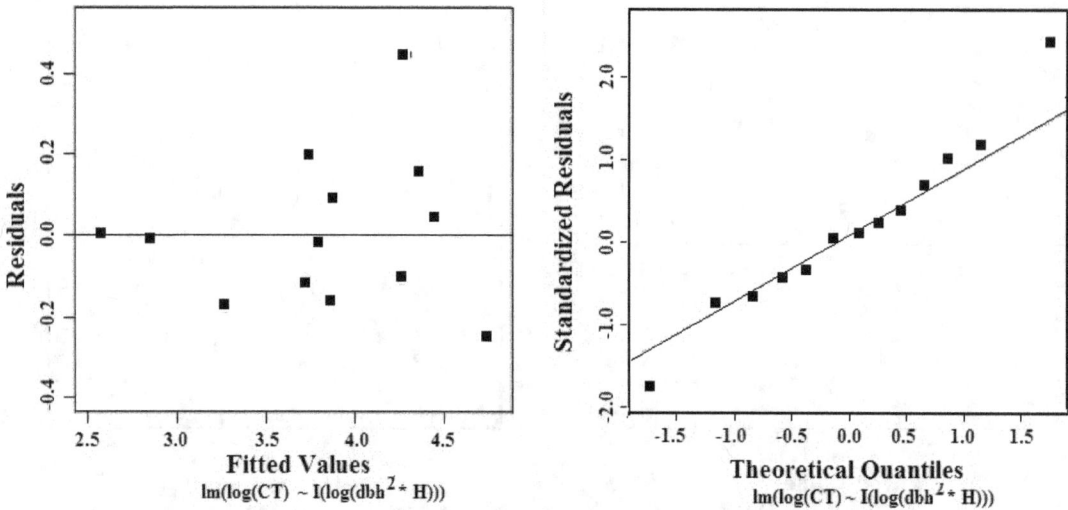

Figure 26. Residuals plotted against fitted values (left) and diagram quantile-quantile (right) for simple linear regression ln (TC) against ln (dbh2H) applied to the species *S. mahagoni*, in plantations established in La Sierra.

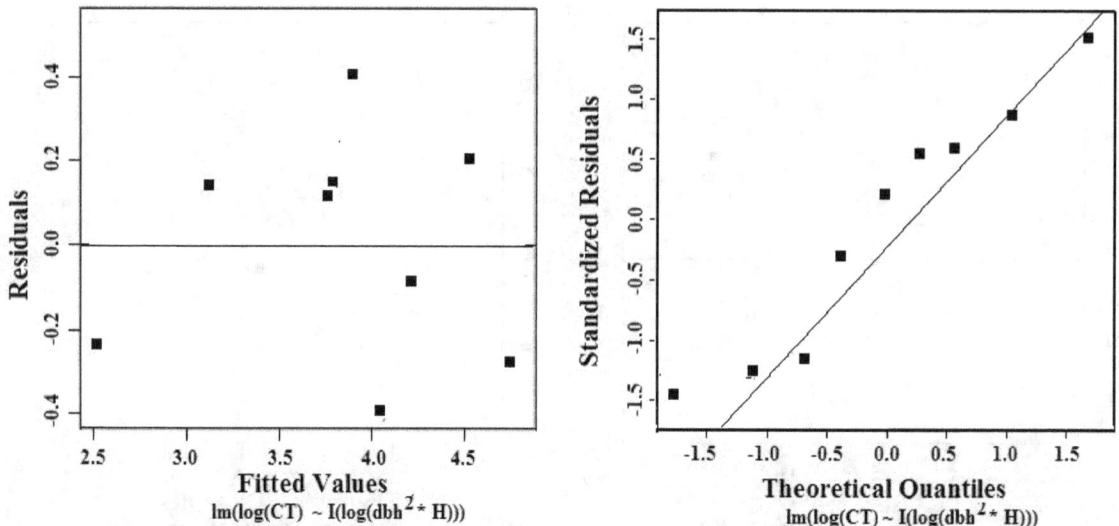

Figure 27. Residuals plotted against fitted values (left panels) and diagram quantile - quantile (right panels) for simple linear regression ln (TC) against ln (dbh2H) applied to the species *S. macrophylla*, in plantations established in La Sierra.
3.6.4 Polynomial regression between ln (TC) and ln (dbh)

We can ask ourselves whether the relationship between ln (TC) and ln (dbh) is actually linear, or is more complex in form. To verify this, we built a second order polynomial regression with dbh as the independent variable. The parameterization of the resulting equations for the species under study is shown in Table 29.

Table 29. Coefficients and corresponding fit statistics using second order polynomial regression between ln (TC) and ln((dbh^{2}H) for the estimation of aerial carbon in *P. occidentalis*, *P. caribaea*, *S. mahagoni* and *S. macrophylla*.

Species	Parameters	Coefficients	Standard Error	t	Pr(>|t|)	AIC
	Intercept	-13.290	4.533	-2.932	0.013	
P. occidentalis	log(dbh)	9.735	3.241	3.003	0.011	-1.791
	log(dbh)2	-1.309	0.574	-2.281	0.042	
P. caribaea	Coefficients no statistically significant (Valor P < 0.05)					
S. mahagoni	Coefficients no statistically significant (Valor P < 0.05)					
S. macrophylla	Coefficients no statistically significant (Valor P < 0.05)					

It can be seen that this second order polynomial regression between ln (TC) and ln (dbh) was only statistically significant for *P. occidentalis*. Intercept and slope coefficients for this species are statistically significant (P-value < 0.05), the standard error of the residuals is 0.1952 with 12 degrees of freedom (df), the coefficient of multiple determination, R2 is 0.94, and the F statistic is 101.5 with 2-12 df.

The logarithmic equation and its respective transformation by means of the inverse function of exponentiation obtained for this species using polynomial regression of the dependent variable TC and the independent variable (dbh) is presented below in Table 30.

Table 30. Logarithmic equation and its respective transformation by means of the inverse function of exponentiation obtained for this species using polynomial regression of the independent variable TC and the dependent dbh.

Specie	Logaríthmic Equation	Model
P. occidentalis	$ln(TC) = -13.2904 + 9.7353\,ln(DAP)$ $- 1.3098\,(DAP^2)$	[3]
	Exponential Transformation **	
	$CT = 0.00000169\,(DAP)^{9.7353}(DAP^2)^{-1.3098}$	[3.1]

** Allows for estimations in original scale of the data.

The residual versus fitted plot for linear regression hypothesis tests (Figure 28) do not show improvement. The Q-Q plot shows a better structure, nonetheless, the presence of an extreme value at the beginning and another at the end are conspicuous. We will consider the hypothesis of simple linear regression met moderately.

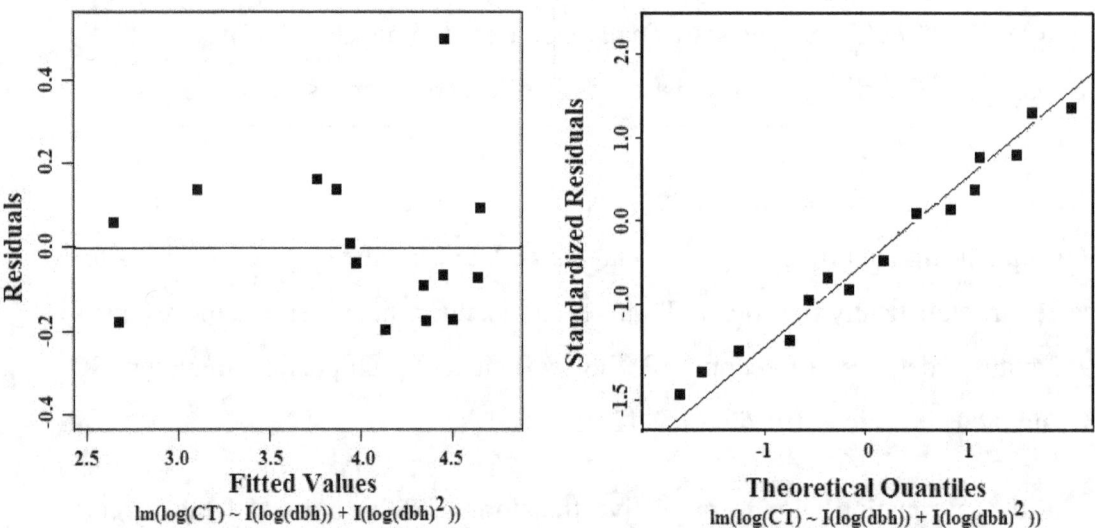

Figure 28. Residuals plotted against fitted values (left panel) and Quantile-Quantile plot (right panel) of the polynomial regression of ln (TC) against ln (dbh2) for 15 trees of *P. occidentalis* in plantations established in La Sierra.

3.6.5 Multiple regression between ln(TC) and ln(dbh), ln(H)

Another possible model is that of a multiple regression considering as separate terms the independent variables dbh and H. Working with data transformed logarithmically to stabilize the residual variance, a multiple regression of ln (TC) against ln (dbh) and total tree height (H) was fitted to the four species, using the method of ordinary least squares. The parameterized model was $(B) = b_o + b_1 \ln(D) + b_2 \ln(H) + \varepsilon$. The resulting equations for the species under study is shown in Table 31.

Table 31. Coefficients and corresponding fit statistics of the data using multiple regression between ln (TC), ln (dbh) and ln (H) for the estimation of aerial carbon in *P. occidentalis*, *P. caribaea*, *S. mahagoni* and *S. macrophylla*.

Species	Parameters	Coefficients	Standard Error	t	Pr(>|t|)	AIC
P. occidentalis	Coefficient for ln (*H*) no statistically significant (Valor P < 0.05). Equation is the same as model [1].					
P. caribaea	Coefficient for ln (*H*) no statistically significant (Valor P < 0.05). Equation is the same as model [4].					
S. mahagoni	Coefficient for ln (*H*) no statistically significant (Valor P < 0.05). Equation is the same as model [6].					
S. macrophylla	Intercept	-4.055	0.423	-9.586	<0.000	
	log(dbh)	1.987	0.270	7.357	<0.000	-0.694
	log(H)	0.902	0.304	2.969	0.025	

S. macrophylla is the only species where the multiple regression model between ln (TC), ln (dbh) and ln (H) has coefficients statistically significant (value p < 0.05). 0.1828 with 6 degrees of freedom, a standard error of residuals of 0.1828, a coefficient of multiple determination R2 is 0.98, and the F statistic is 170.2 with 2 and 6 df.

Table 32, presents the multiple regression equation and its respective transformation by means of the inverse function of exponentiation obtained for this species, regressing the dependent variable TC and the independent variables ln (dbh) and ln (H).

Table 32. Multiple regression equation and its respective transformation by means of the inverse function of exponentiation obtained for *S. macrophylla*, using regression of the dependent variable ln(TC) and the independent variables (dbh) and ln (H).

Specie	Logarithmic Equation	Model
S. macrophylla	$ln(CT) = -4.0546 + 1.9874\ ln(DAP) + ln(H)$	[10]
	Exponential Transformation **	
	$CT = 0.01734\ (DAP)^{1.9874} * (H)^{0.9021}$	[10.1.1]

** Allows for estimations in original scale of the data.

3.6.6 Recommended models to estimate total carbon in *P. occidentalis*, *P. caribaea*, *S. mahagoni* and *S. macrophylla*.

Based on the goodness-of-fit statistics (Table 33), we recommend that to estimate aerial total carbon captured by the species planted by Plan Sierra, the following models (equations) be use:

Species	Model	Equation
P. occidentalis	[1.1]	$TC = 0.0493\ dbh^{2.3504}$
P. caribaea	[4.1]	$TC = 0.0111\ dbh^{2.8581}$
S. mahagoni	[6.1]	$TC = 0.0413\ dbh^{2.4887}$
S. macrophylla	[8.1]	$TC = 0.0234\ dbh^{2.6619}$
	[10.1]	$TC = 0.0173\ dbh^{1.9874} H^{0.9021}$

Table 33. Goodness-of-fit statistics of the suggested equations [1.1] [4.1] [6.1] [8.1] and [10.1] to estimate the aerial total carbon in the main species used by Plan Sierra in their reforestation programs.

Species	Equation	RMSE	BIAS	MGD	R2	AIC
P. occidentalis	[1.1]	4.06	0.265	10.373	0.92	1.613
P. caribaea	[4.1]	4.71	1.962	12.972	0.97	0.308
S. mahagoni	[6.1]	10.67	-2.271	20.634	0.96	7.394
S. macrophylla	[8.1]	3.18	-2.366	7.902	0.96	5.439
	[10.1]	3.92	-1.244	8.479	0.98	-0.694

RMSE: Root Mean Squared Error; MGD: Mean Global Deviation; R2: Coefficient of Determination; AIC: Akaike Information Criteria

Equations [1.1] and [4.1] overestimate aerial total carbon content by 0.265 and 1.962 kilograms, respectively. Equations [6.1], [8.1] and [10.1] underestimate it by 2.271, 2.366 and 1.244 kilograms, respectively.

Based on these equations, carbon content for each species and age class would be obtained by inserting into each specific model of the corresponding species, the value of the diameter at breast height (dbh, 1.30 m) to the tree being evaluated. For the studied stands, the average quantities of dbh, and H of the tree, total trees per hectare, aerial total carbon per tree, carbon content obtained by applying the corresponding equation and carbon dioxide equivalent (CO_2_equivalente) captured for each age class evaluated are presented in Table 34, for the pine species and Table 35 for the mahoganies.

Table 34. Average values of dbh and tree total height (H); total of trees per hectare, aerial total carbon per tree, carbon content obtained by applying the corresponding equation for each species and carbon dioxide equivalent (CO2_equivalente) stored for each age class in pine species.

Species	Age Class (Years)	Averaged dbh (cm)	Averaged Total H (m)	Trees per Hectare (No.)	Aerial Total Carbon per Tree (Kg)	Aerial Total Carbon per Hectare (Kg)	CO2 Equivalent (Kg)
P. occidentalis	2	12.26	10.67	1,943	19.80	38,461.65	141,154.26
	3	17.00	14.33	571	40.29	23,021.75	84,489.82
	4	19.38	15.41	1,057	60.91	64,386.63	236,298.93
	5	21.93	16.82	857	78.16	66,997.41	245,880.49
	6	23.56	17.35	543	78.71	47,729.38	175,166.82
	7	17.00	14.22	571	41.66	23,807.65	87,374.08
P. caribaea	1	6.80	4.08	571	2.83	1,620.2	5,946.13
	2	13.21	11.82	3,771	21.24	80,106.34	293,990.27
	3	21.44	18.07	514	72.79	37,434.83	137,385.83
	4	20.58	17.45	1,371	67.61	92,718.20	340,275.79
	5	23.22	18.77	1,857	98.91	183,681.17	674,109.89
	6	29.50	21.06	114	219.75	25,114.91	92,171.72
	7	25.57	20.09	1,000	125.83	125,826.39	461,782.85

Table 35. Average values of dbh and tree total height (H); total of trees per hectare, aerial total carbon per tree, carbon content obtained by applying the corresponding equation for each species and carbon dioxide equivalent (CO2_equivalente) stored for each age class in mahogany species.

Species	Age Class (Years)	Averaged dbh (cm)	Averaged Total H (m)	Trees per Hectare (No.)	Aerial Total Carbon per Tree (Kg)	Aerial Total Carbon per Hectare (Kg)	CO2 Equivalent (Kg)
S. mahagoni	1	4.67	4.97	514	2.14	1,102.66	4,046.76
	2	7.87	6.53	1,114	7.80	8,692.81	31,902.61
	3	7.36	6.22	314	7.66	2,407.49	8,835.49
	4	21.00	9.52	1,600	19.72	31,555.34	115,808.10
	5	13.76	8.16	600	31.56	18,935.96	69,494.97
	6	21.00	9.40	171	91.91	15,576.28	57,164.95
	7	20.08	9.25	1,057	84.54	89,373.54	328,000.89
S. macrophylla	1	7.44	6.25	771	5.43	4,191.21	15,381.74
	2	17.55	11.79	943	50.08	47,221.11	173,301.47
	3	13.61	10.14	943	26.30	24,796.62	91,003.60
	4	17.91	11.59	1,514	69.14	104,545.60	383,682.35

4 Conclusions

To assess biomass and carbon stock, and at the same time develop allometric models for species chosen by Plan Sierra as pillars of their reforestation programs, 52 stands of artificial plantations were inventoried: 15 of *Pinus caribaea* var. Caribaea; 15 of *Pinus occidentalis*; 13 of *Swietenia mahagoni* (small leave mahagoni), and 9 *of Swietenia macrophylla* (big leave mahogany). A study program was developed where a specific number of trees for different age classes should be sampled. There were difficulties in locating representative trees for each class and the destructive sampling was not executed according to the established plans. For example, in *P. occidentalis* it was assumes that there would be 2 trees in age classes 1 to 3, and 3 trees in age classes 4 to 6. However, there were no trees representing class 1; in class 4 trees were evaluated and there was a tree out of the age classes perceived.

A silvicultural and allometric characterization of the 52 sampled stands was performed. Hence forward, values of the variables are reports in the following order: *P. occidentalis*, *P. caribaea*, S. mahagoni and *S. macrophylla*, respectively. The assessed stands are on average, 19, 19, 23 and 16 years old; the average area in hectares for the order established is 1.64, 2.47, 1.52 and 1.55; the number of trees per hectare was 273, 586, 543 and 436; volume including bark was 37.72, 130.0, 36.6 and 45.16 cubic meters. Discriminating by age, average dbh (cm) was 18.52, 20.05, 16.68 and 14.13. The average total height (m) was 15.91, 14.80, 9.94, and 7.72. Considering the trees sampled individually, aerial total carbon (Kg) averaged per tree was 86.99, 53.26 and 37.74, 35.05.

Average aerial total carbon (Kg / has) of assessed stands and discriminating by age-class was 44,064.41; 78,071.72; 23,949.15 and 45,188.64. The respective average per age-class of $CO2\_equivalente$ (Kg / has) was of 161,727.40; 286,523.21; 87,893.40 and 165,842.29. The species with the greatest amount of carbon stored at the stand level is *P. caribaea*, with 86.99 Kg per tree. Individually, the content of carbon, derived by multiplying dry biomass by carbon concentration, is greater in *P. caribaea*, and therefore its capture of $CO2$ equivalent is higher on average (365.81 kg).

An analysis of variance (Table 24) shows that the concentration of carbon in the branches is statistically significant and greater in *P. occidentalis* as compared to both mahoganies, although biomass content for this species is lower than for *P. caribaea*. Carbon concentration in branches of *P. caribaea* is statistically significant and larger than the equivalent for *S. macrophylla*. The foliage of *P. occidentalis* has higher concentration of carbon in the foliage than *S. macrophylla*.

Individual consideration of the 52 trees shows that, stem density averaged at three relative heights (0.1, 0.5 and 0.8) was respectively 0.48, 0.44, 0.58, and 0.52. The relationship dry-weight / fresh-weight in the stem was 0.52, 0.46, 0.64, and 0.59, respectively. In branches, samples taken at three positions within the canopy had a dry-weight / fresh-weight relationship of 0.48 0.49 0.53 and 0.53 respectively. In the foliage this ratio was 0.49, 0.46, 0.46, and 0.47.

For *P. occidentalis* sample trees of, the average global amounts by age class of dbh (cm), H (m), aerial dry biomass (kg), aerial total C content, (kg) and the $CO2\_equivalente$ (kg) were, respectively: 19.82, 15.13, 152.96, 59.67 and 218.99. For *P. caribaea* these quantities were: 23.76, 18.51, 287.71, 149.39 and 548.28. In *S. mahagoni* 15.51, 8.54, 122.91, 48.63 and 189.28. For *S. mahagoni* 16.37, 10.97, 132.05, 51.57 and 189.28.

It was expected to find an increase in biomass positively correlated with age, however, the "sample" trees assessed are not representative of all the variability in terms of age class. The amount of biomass accumulated and therefore carbon captured is directly proportional to the size of the tree.

In addition to evaluating biomass and carbon in the species, different relationships including, those between dbh, total tree height and volume including bark of trees sampled in temporary plots were considered. The relationship between dbh and H is better described by a logarithmic relationship. The best fit for dbh vs H is found *for P. caribaea*, followed by *S. macrophylla*, *P. occidentalis*, and lastly for *S. mahagoni*.

To develop the allometric models, four models were fitted in order to establish the relationship between the dependent variable 'aerial total carbon' and the predicting variables, dbh, H and dbh2H. For each type of model the method of least squares was employed, by applying logarithmic transformations, which allows to correct the problem of linearity and heteroscedasticity inherent to this type of biological variables. The inverse exponential function was used to express models developed in original scale units of the data.

Recommended models to estimate aerial total carbon in the species evaluated, based on the fitting and age classes studied are as follows:

For *P. occidentalis*, model [1.1];

For *P. caribaea*, model [4.1];

For *S. mahagoni*, model [6.1];

For *S. macrophylla*, models [8.1] and [10.1];

Models containing a single independent variable are [1.1], [4.1], [6.1] and [8.1]. They are simpler and easily applied.

5 References

Bueno-López, S.W.; E. Bevilacqua; Torres-Herrera, J.G.; Garcia-Lucas, E.; Caraballo-Rojas, L.R. 2018. Site-specific Allometric Equations for Total Aboveground Dry Biomass and Carbon Content of Naturally Regenerated *Pinus occidentalis* Sw. Trees. (no publicado)

Burger H, 1945. Holz, Blattmenge und Zuwachs. VII: Die Lärche. In: Forest mensuration (Van Laar A, Akça A, eds, 1997). Cuvillier, Göttingen, Germany. Mitt Schw Anst fd Forstl Versw 24: 7-103.

Burger H, 1953. Holz, Blattmenge und Zuwachs. XIII: Fichten im gleichaltrigen Hochwald (Van Laar A, Akça A, eds, 1997). Mitt Schw Anst Forstl Versuchsw 29: 38-130.

Canga, E.; Dieguez-Aranda, I.; Afif-Khouri, E.; Camara-Obregon, A. 2013. Aboveground biomass equations for *Pinus radiata* D. Don in Asturias. Forest Systems, 22 (3): 408-415.   – doi: 10.5424/fs/2013223-04143

Chaturvedi, R.K. and Raghubanshi, A.S. 2015. Allometric Models for Accurate Estimation of Aboveground Biomass of Teak in Tropical Dry Forests of India. For. Sci. 61 (5) 938–949 – doi: http://dx.doi.org/10.5849/forsci.14-190

Dickinson, Y.L. and Zenner, E.K. 2010. Allometric Equations for the Aboveground Biomass of Selected Common Eastern Hardwood Understory Species. North. J. Appl. For. 27 (4) 160-165.

Elias, M.and Potvin, C. Assessing inter- and intra-specific variation in trunk carbon concentration for 32 neotropical tree species. Can. J. For. Res. 2003, 33, 1039–1045.

Fonseca, W.; Alice, F.E.; and Rey-Benayas, J.M. 2012. Carbon accumulation in aboveground and belowground biomass and soil of different age native forest plantations in the humid tropical lowlands of Costa Rica. New Forest 43:197–211

LiYong, F.; WeiSheng, Z.; and ShouZheng, T. 2016. Mean prediction errors of aboveground biomass models for the species were less than 5%, except for Yunnan pine. For. Sci. 63 (3) 241–249. https://doi.org/10.5849/FS-2016-055.

Gifford, R.M. 1994. The global carbon cycle, a viewpoint on the missing sink. Aust. J. Plant Physiol. 21: 1–15.

IPCC (Intergovernmental Panel on Climate Change). 2003. Report on good practice guidance for land use, land-use change and forestry. IPCC National Greenhouse Gas Inventories Programme (http://www.ipcc-nggip.iges.or.jp/public/gpglulucf/gpglulucf.htm), Japan.

Lamlom, S.H.; Savidge, R.A. 2003. A reassessment of carbon content in wood: Variation within and between 41 North American species. Biomass Bioenergy. 25, 381–388.

Picard, N.; Saint-André, L. and Henry, M. 2012. Manual for building tree volume and biomass allometric equations from field measurement to prediction. Centre de Coopération Internationale en Recherche Agronomique pour le Développement and Forestry Department Food and Agriculture Organization of the United Nations. 207 pp.

Thomas, S.C. and Malczewski, G. 2007. Wood carbon content of tree species in eastern China: Interspecific variability and the importance of the volatile fraction. J. Environ. Manag. 2007, 85, 659–662.

Thomas, S.C. and Martin, A.R. 2012. Carbon Content of Tree Tissues: A Synthesis. Forests, Vol 3, 332-352; doi:10.3390/f3020332.

ABOUT THE AUTHOR

Dr. S.W. Bueno currently leads the Silviculture, Environment and Climate Change Research program at Pontificia Universidad Catolica Madre y Maestra. Has expertise in quantitative silviculture with more than 10 years of experience in forest research, extension and teaching. He completed a Bachelor's of Science degree in Agronomy (focused on forest resources management) at the Pontificia Universidad Católica Madre y Maestra (PUCMM, Dominican Republic). After, he completed a Master's of Science degree in Forest Resources Management (focused on nursery soils) from the State University of New York, College of Environmental Science and Forestry (SUNY_ESF) at Syracuse, New York, USA. He came back to SUNY_ESF to obtain a Ph.D. in Quantitative Silviculture, focused on the modeling growth and yield of forest stands and individual trees.